SWITCH CRAFT

BATTERY-POWERED CRAFTS TO MAKE AND SEW

ALISON LEWIS WITH FANG-YU LIN

PHOTOGRAPHY BY HEATHER WESTON

TECHNICAL ILLUSTRATIONS BY HIROMI SUGIE

POTTER CRAFT

NEW YORK

This book is dedicated to my loving family, who told me I could do anything I put my mind to. This book wouldn't exist without you believing in me and all my crazy ideas.

— Alison

....

To my family.

— Fang-Yu

Copyright © 2008 by Alison Lewis and Fang-Yu Lin
Photographs copyright © 2008 by Heather Weston

All rights reserved.

Published in the United States by Potter Craft, an imprint of the Crown Publishing Group, a division of Random House, Inc., New York.
www.crownpublishing.com
www.pottercraft.com

POTTER CRAFT and colophon is a registered trademark of Random House, Inc.

Library of Congress Cataloging-in-Publication Data

Lewis, Alison, 1974–
  Switch craft : battery-powered crafts to make and sew / Alison Lewis with Fang-Yu Lin. — 1st ed.
    p. cm.
  Includes bibliographical references and index.
  ISBN-13: 978-0-307-39544-3
  1. Machine sewing. 2. Electronic apparatus and appliances. I. Lin, Fang-Yu. II. Title.
  TT713.L49 2008
  646.2'044—dc22   2008007198

ISBN: 978-0-307-39544-3

Printed in China

Design by La Tricia Watford
Technical Illustrations by Hiromi Sugie

10 9 8 7 6 5 4 3 2 1

First Edition

POTTER CRAFT NEWSLETTER:
Sign up for our monthly newsletter at www.pottercraft.com to get information about new books, receive free patterns, and enter contests to win prizes.

CONTENTS

"Don't be afraid to use your imagination and really launch out into the deep. Then, who knows what you may come up with. Nothing has been made that's worthwhile without someone having a vision. May yours be great!"

—Alice Merryman

INTRODUCTION

As a small girl, I'd tinker with the family phone and tear open my Teddy Ruxpin. These devices seemed magical, and I wondered what they were all about. Everything inside looked beautiful but strange. I wanted to learn how it all worked but didn't have anyone to teach me. I still remember wanting a spectacular skirt that would light up the night when I twirled. I knew the skirt was easy enough to sew, but how was I ever going to put shimmering lights into it? At the time it seemed impossible, so I tried to forget about it. Years later, after learning electronics in graduate school, I looked back to that that frustrated girl wanting her shimmering skirt and thought, not is only is it time to make the skirt for myself, but it's time to teach others how to do the same.

Enter *Switch Craft*. In this twenty-project book, I am going to show you how to make the skirt that sparkles, sophisticated bags that integrate speakers for your MP3 player, and even a pillow that functions as a telephone, so you can snuggle up for late night chats in comfort.

Sound scary? Well, it isn't. For me, I just had to get over my fears, which stemmed from the antiquated idea that taking a shop or electronics class meant social suicide. But now we are in the age of the cool hip techie diva who loves Gucci as well as her cell phone. There is nothing holding us back from working with electronics and craft except for a few fears of our own, and that is what this book will remedy.

To do this, *Switch Craft* won't bore you with electronic geek speak. Instead, I focus on recognizable language and skills you already know and have—through sewing and craft—and apply them to projects that matter to you. These projects incorporate your traditional sewing skills while at the same time allowing you to see their value outside of the traditional craft medium.

In this book you'll use your skills to make items that are both beautiful and useful by integrating light, vibration, and sound. You've never done anything like this before! Well, if you have, it was in sixth-grade science class, and the project was probably a blinking light—whoop-de-doo! Now you can do something worthwhile with that flickering light—like making your cell phone shine when it rings or illuminating a message on a fashionable clutch.

This book is for those who want to empower themselves and take their sewing and crafting skills to the next level. If there is any part of you that is hesitant to proceed, I encourage you to approach it like you would any other sewing or craft project, and trust your skills. Being a smart sewer and crafter, you certainly won't find the topic alien just because the project uses a few new materials from what you see in typical craft books. It is my hope that you'll find it is not hard at all—it's just a different set of words and some new rules here and there. You'll see that a pattern is just a pattern and a diagram is just a diagram. You work with things like thread, beads, and needles all the time, so threading a little lighted bead onto some wire should be no stretch at all!

—Alison Lewis

HOW TO USE THIS BOOK

WHAT YOU NEED TO KNOW ABOUT SEWING

This book uses basic sewing jargon and references to techniques such as topstitching and buttonholes. Familiarity with a sewing machine, hand-sewing, or beading is a big plus. However, if you are new to sewing (or a little rusty), there is no reason why you can't make these projects. Grab a friend who sews and make the projects together, or try out one of the projects that requires only a few simple stitches like the Dancing Queen Skirt (page 25) or the Whisper Charm (page 34).

WHAT YOU NEED TO KNOW ABOUT ELECTRONICS

You don't have to know anything about electronics. We have made sure that every project uses introductory electronic skills. Nothing in this book is beyond the level of a sixth-grade science class. The Basics sections (page 102) will prep those who have never worked with battery-powered electronics and will provide a refresher course for those who have. Dive in to the life-changing excitement in making something come alive, light up, or tickle your fancy.

STRUCTURE OF THE BOOK

You've probably figured out that *Switch Craft* is not your typical sewing book. To help guide you, we've put together killer Basic Materials, Basic Tools, and Basic Skills sections, along with Basic Elements, Glossary and Reference sections. We suggest you start by reading the Basic Switch Materials (page 102) and Basic Switch Skills (page 109) sections, where you'll learn techniques that will endow you with sewing and technology prowess. Then, take a peek at the Basic Switch Elements section (page 115) to familiarize yourself with all the tantalizing tricks that will make your project light up, move, or make noise.

In the Basic Elements section, you'll learn to make your own electronic parts from commonly found craft and sewing materials. This is a unique section, as these parts are meant not only for the projects in this book, but for your own crafted items as well.

Once you learn how to make your own soft and interactive electronic parts, there is no limit to what you can do! Add what you learn here to your own creations and see just how far you can take them.

After familiarizing yourself with the Basics sections, it's time to start the projects. There are twenty projects designed to show off your originality, smarts, and charm, or to entertain your furry pal. They are broken down into themed chapters that play off commonalities found in both fashion and electronic products. Within each project there is a materials list, illustrations, instructions, use and care suggestions, and a "remix" section:

• The materials list has everything you need to make your project work, including fabrics, notions, electrical parts, references to the pattern pieces in the back of the book, and any special tools. Sometimes in the materials list we ask you to build a part from the Basic Elements.

• The instructions and illustrations are meant to work together. You'll see a marked letter in parentheses (A) in the instructions whenever we refer you to a drawing. Some illustrations show how your item should look after it's created, others show multiple steps all in one illustration, and still others are diagrams for the electronic components.

• The use and care section is just that: It lets you know how to use your new responsive design and tells you how to care for its fabrics and electronics.

• The "remix" section found at the end of each project provides suggestions on how to take your project further by adding to its design or creating your own unique variation.

Within each project, look for the fun facts we've added to enlighten you on how electronics have affected our lives and how the technology works. Let these sidebars inspire you to seek out and make your own creations and to think about how you relate to and use technology every day.

ICONS AND SYMBOLS

 CAUTION: Pay special attention to the caution icon; it indicates possible dangers in the circuit or construction.

IMPORTANT: The important icon refers you to special techniques or tools.

TIP: The tip icon has helpful hints and reminders about sewing techniques, using special fabrics, or alternatives to tools and techniques.

[CRAFT]

The craft level icon symbolizes the level of sewing or crafting skill required for a project. A simple project, indicated with only one craft icon, requires a minimal amount of sewing and crafting, like simple stitching and stuffing. The most challenging projects may require many different stitch types and techniques and advanced sewing and craft knowledge, such as pattern alterations and preparing unique fabrics.

[TECH]

The tech level icon specifies the level of electrical knowledge or skill you'll need to complete the project. It ranges from the easiest, which contains no soldering or electronics at all, to the most challenging, which means soldering multiple joints, working with small or delicate parts, or opening up an off-the-shelf electronic product.

[COST]

The cost level icon is our best estimate of how much each project costs to make. In this number we include the price of the technology, extra craft items and sewing notions such as buttons and zippers, and fabric. Your cost will vary relative to where you live and how much you spend on fabrics.

[+]

The plus symbol is used throughout the instructions and illustrations to indicate the positive or plus side of your power source.

[−]

The minus symbol is used throughout the instructions and illustrations to indicate the negative or ground side of your power source.

COMPANION SITE

Our companion website is located at www.iheartswitch.com/switchcraft. Go to the website to see updated resources, helpful guides and how-tos, and more projects to challenge the Switch Crafter in you.

BE SMART, STAY SAFE!

We want you to challenge yourself, but that doesn't mean throwing caution to the wind. Like with any craft, use common sense and take precautions. To help you, we've put together some special safety measures for working with electronics.

....

• Read the Basics sections (page 102). They have all the information you'll need to understand the parts and techniques commonly used in electronics.

• Read all the directions before starting each project. This way, any questions can be addressed before starting, preventing possible misunderstandings and mishaps.

• We've worked hard to put together the best selection of electronic products you'll need for a beautifully working project. Try to get the exact item we suggest in the materials list; if you can't, we've listed alternatives in the Basic Switch Materials section.

• Fashion doesn't need to be hazardous. Be safe when working with electronics by pulling your hair back and removing all jewelry. Your hair and jewelry can get caught while you're working, and metal jewelry can create short circuits.

• Create a safe workspace by working on wood or other nonconductive material. If you're not sure about your workspace table, work on a wooden cutting board. Remember that a cutting board that's been soldered upon should never be used for food prep.

• Keep batteries away from heat. This includes never soldering wires or anything else directly to a battery, as this could cause the battery to overheat and possibly explode.

• Always remove the battery or power source before working with electronics.

• Be careful of short circuits. The electrical part of the projects won't hurt you; you're more likely to hurt them by creating a short circuit. You're not working with a large amount of electricity, but your batteries won't take kindly to having their wires being crossed, and neither will you. Short circuits can damage the battery and the project and can cause sparks, fire, and in extreme cases, explosions, which isn't any fun, especially not next to fabric (yikes!). To prevent

a short circuit, never let the exposed [+] and [−] wires or conductive threads of your project cross or touch.

• Watch out for sharp edges. You may be working with metal and cut plastic. Trim all sharp edges down with a nail file.

• When you can, use natural fabrics, and always use natural fabrics next to electronic parts. We've all seen toys be recalled by the manufacturer, and often this is because they don't use safe materials or fabrics. We suggest using natural fibers and materials like cotton or linen, since synthetic fabrics may contain unknown chemicals that heat up with the electronics—don't endanger your health (or your pet's!).

• The rosin in the solder releases fumes when heated that may be harmful to your eyes and lungs. We suggest using lead-free solder. When soldering, work in a well-ventilated area and protect your eyes with plastic goggles.

• Always wash your hands after using solder.

• If you may become pregnant, are pregnant, or are nursing, do not work with solder—even lead-free solder—or handle electrical components. You can change batteries and make projects with off-the-shelf components like a voice recorder, but no soldering or making electrical stuff!

• Never touch the tip of a hot soldering iron. Once you turn it off, wait for it to cool down completely before replacing the iron tip or putting it away.

IMPORTANT: Although every reasonable effort has been made to ensure the accuracy and reliability of the information and instructions contained in this book, the success and safety in creating these projects depends on individual care and judgment. The author and publisher expressly disclaim any liability, loss, or risk, personal or otherwise, which is incurred as a consequence, directly or indirectly, of the use and application of any of the contents of this book.

Chapter One: Show Off

Designs that shine a light on you!

SEAT GLOWS WHEN SAT UPON

cushion brite

Unlike Lite-Brite, Cushion Brite is both colorful and comfy. Living life by the seat of your pants has never been easier. Sit down and watch the neon trim glow! Use Cushion Brite as a cool party favor at your next soirée or add an accent of light to your décor.

[CRAFT] ■ ■ ▢   [TECH] ■ ■ ▢   [COST] ■ ▢ ▢

[MATERIALS & TOOLS]

FABRIC A: 1 yd (0.9m) of medium- to heavy-weight fabric, such as cotton or linen

Two pieces Bias Strip Tape, each 65¼" (1.66m) long

½" (13mm) wide sew-on Velcro, 27½" (70cm) long

All-purpose thread to match fabric

5mm-wide EL wire. 10' (3m) long in the color of your choice

EL wire driver (page 105)

Donut Switch (page 119). This will require a round

pottery sponge and conductive fabric, same size as pottery sponge

Cotton stuffing

Two complementary buttons

Core tools (page 106)

PATTERN SCHEMATIC (page 132)

CUT THE PATTERN

1. Cut out two Cushion Surfaces, two Side Velcro Panels, and one Side Panel from fabric A. Cut two 13¾" (34.9cm) Velcro strips.

2. Make two 65¼" (1.66m) bias strip tubes by pressing the bias tape open, folding it in half lengthwise, and stitching about ⅜" (1cm) from the fold, leaving the ends open. The depth of your seam may change depending on the diameter of the EL wire you purchase. Check to make sure the EL wire can be easily inserted into the diameter of your tube.

3. Cut out two round pieces from the conductive fabric in the same size and shape of the pottery sponge.

MAKE THE SIDE PANEL

4. Sew one Velcro strip onto the right side of each Side Panel, as marked **(A)**. Join the Velcro together and sew the Velcro Side Panels together at the notches **(B)**.

5. Lay the Velcro Side Panel flat and press the seam allowance and Velcro closure to one side.

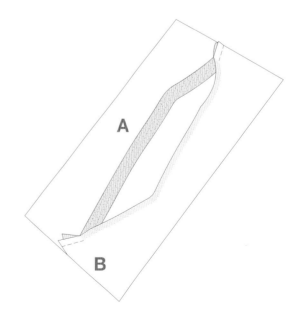

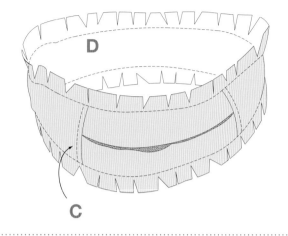

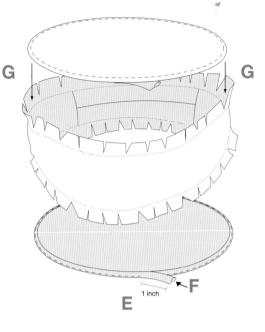

6. With right sides together, sew the ends of the Side Panel to the Velcro Side Panel with a ½" (13mm) seam **(C)**.

7. Clip into the seam allowance every inch around the Cushion Side Panel top and bottom edges. This makes it easier to turn right side out later and easier to sew multiple layers **(D)**.

ADD THE BIAS STRIP TUBES

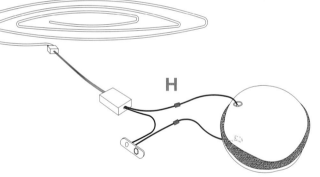

8. Pin one Bias Strip Tube to the right side of one Cushion Surface, matching raw edges. The Tube will be facing towards the center of the Cushion Surface.

9. Begin sewing at the seam line of the bias strip, leaving the end of the Tube open. Sew the Bias Strip Tube around the Cushion Surface to meet the other end **(E)**. Do not sew through either end of the Bias Strip Tube. Leave them open for EL wire to be inserted later **(F)**.

10. Repeat steps 8 and 9 for the other Cushion Surface.

11. With right sides together, pin and sew the Cushion Surfaces to each side of the Side Panel. Do not sew over the open ends of the Bias Strip Tubes **(G)**. This will leave a small opening in the side, which you'll sew together later.

↻ remix

- Try changing the shape of the cushion.
- Play with multiple tubes or different light combinations.
- Try a blinking or sound-responsive EL wire driver.

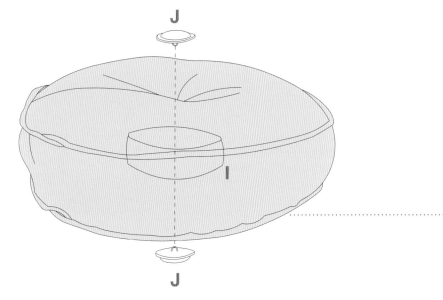

J

I

J

USE & CARE

>> Remove the EL driver and battery before washing. Reinstall them only after the cushion completely dries.

>> When the light becomes dim, replace the battery.

PREPARE THE EL WIRE AND SWITCH

12. Use the pottery sponge and the two conductive fabric pieces to create a Donut Switch with two wires (page 119).

13. Cut the red wire of the EL Wire driver between the battery snap and the plastic case.

14. Following the diagram, solder the two wires from the Donut Switch to the ends of the cut red wire (H).

15. Cover the solder joints with electrical tape and connect the EL wire to the driver. Snap on the battery and test the switch. (The light should turn on when you press the Donut Switch).

PUT IT ALL TOGETHER

16. Turn the cushion right side out. Insert the EL wire into the Bias Strip Tube through one opening and push it all the way around to the opposite open end. Continue threading the EL Wire all the way through the other Bias Strip Tube.

17. Stuff the cushion to about 90% full.

18. Place the Donut Switch inside the cushion at the center (I).

19. Put the driver, battery, and any excess EL Wire into the cushion near the Velcro opening. Finish stuffing.

20. Slip stitch the openings around the Tubes shut.

21. Sew one button to the center of one of the Cushion Surfaces. Don't cut your thread. String it through the opposite side of the cushion passing it through the Donut Switch to keep it secure. Pull the thread to the other side, tightly, and sew on the other button to the opposite Cushion center (J). Be careful not to sew it too tight or you'll activate your Donut Switch.

BLINKS WHEN
RECEIVING CALLS

Never miss a call again because your cell phone is buried deep in your bag and you can't hear it ringing. With the Antenna Bag, you have a sophisticated and stylish carryall that will light up when your cell phone rings. No matter what the occasion—be it in class, a business lunch, or a girls' night out—the Antenna Bag can always catch the signal.

antenna bag

[CRAFT] ■ ■ ▢   [TECH] ■ ■ ■   [COST] ■ ■ ▢

[MATERIALS & TOOLS]

FABRIC A, EXTERIOR: 1⅝ yd (1.5m) medium-weight fabric, such as cotton, denim, canvas, or twill

FABRIC B, LINING: 1⅝ yd (1.5m) lightweight fabric such as silk, habiti, charmeuse, or similar synthetic

3" x 3" (7.5cm x 7.5cm) sheer white fabric square

All-purpose thread to match fabrics A and B

Embroidery floss of contrasting color to fabric A

2¼" (5.5cm) long piece of ½" (13mm) wide sew-on Velcro

Call Indicator Set (page 122)

Core tools (page 106)

PATTERN (page 124)

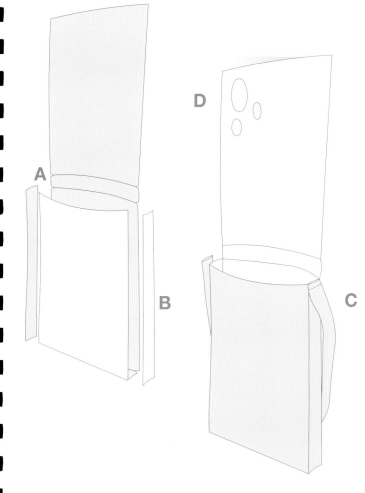

CUT THE PATTERN AND MAKE A PHONE POCKET

1. Cut out 2 Side Panels, 2 Straps, and the Body pieces from fabric A. Cut out 2 Side Panels, the Body, and the Battery Pocket from fabric B. Mark all the symbols and fold lines with a fabric-marking tool.

2. Make a patch pocket for your mobile phone using fabric A (page 109). Sew the phone pocket onto the Bag Body exterior where marked.

CREATE THE BAG BODY AND THE STRAP

3. On the Bag Body, snip into the fabric about ⅜" (9.5mm) on the fold lines. Fold and press the Body at the fold lines to give it a rectangular box shape (A).

4. With right sides together, sew the exterior Side Panels to the Bag Body (B).

5. Create a strap by sewing both Strap pieces with right sides together with a ¼" (6mm) seam, leaving one end open. Turn the Strap right side out, press, and topstitch ⅛" (3mm) from the edges.

6. Baste the Strap to the right sides of Side Panels where marked (C).

7. Cut the three circles from the Bag Body as marked on the pattern (D).

8. Cut three circles out of fabric B that are ½″ (13mm) larger in diameter than the circles that you just cut out from the exterior Bag Body. Use Fray Check to seal the edges.

9. Baste the circles to the back of the circular holes. Following the diagram, make small stitches perpendicular to the circle edge around the circles with your embroidery floss (E).

 TIP: If you are using a fabric that frays excessively, you may need to clip and fold back the edges of the circles to the inside and topstitch them to the pocket.

MAKE THE BAG LINING AND THE BATTERY POCKET

10. Using a zigzag or buttonhole stitch on your sewing machine, create a buttonhole on the Lining Body, as marked, for the Battery Pocket.

11. Make a patch pocket (page 109) from the Lining Battery Pocket piece. Sew one side of the Velcro strip to the Battery Pocket and the other to the Lining Body as marked.

12. Line the Velcro pieces together and topstitch the Battery Pocket onto the Lining Body as marked (F, on opposite page).

13. With right sides together, sew the Lining Side Panels to the Lining Body. You do not need to press and fold the Lining Body.

 TIP: If you are using a lightweight fabric, such as silk, for the Lining, you should interface the Lining and the battery pocket for stability before sewing.

PREPARE THE CALL INDICATOR

14. Follow the instructions on page 122 to create a Call Indicator with 3 light-up circuits. Solder the [+] and [–] wires of the 9-volt battery snap to the respective [+] and [–] wires of your Call Indicator (G).

15. Cut a 3″ (7.5cm) diameter circle out of the sheer fabric square and sew the three circuits of the Call Indicator to the fabric by wrapping and stitching the thread around the wires and the units. Make sure that they are securely fastened (H).

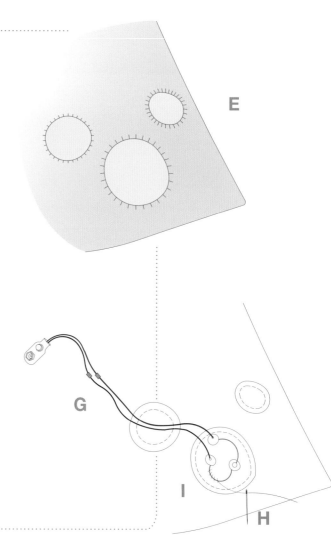

↻ remix

- Add the electronic portion of the Antenna Bag to an existing bag instead of making it from scratch.
- Replace the circles with your own design.
- Modify the bag by attaching an outside pocket or making it smaller.

16. Leaving the battery snap out, hand-sew the fabric piece with the Call Indicator to the Bag Body behind the largest circle, with the lights facing the Bag Body (I).

PUT THE BAG TOGETHER

17. With the Lining Body wrong side out and the Bag Body right side out, place the Bag Body into the Lining Body. Sew around the bag opening and the flap, leaving an opening as marked on the pattern (J).

18. Turn the bag right side out and push the Lining into the bag. Pull the battery snap through the buttonhole on the Lining Body, threading it into the Battery Pocket.

19. Reinforce the strap connection by machine straight stitching around the surfaces where the Strap and the Side Panels meet. Also stitch diagonally across the surfaces. The resulting stitches should look like an X inside a box on both surfaces.

20. To finish, slip stitch the opening closed.

USE & CARE

>> Place your cell phone in the phone pocket, close the flap, and watch your circle illuminate with every incoming call.

>> For cleaning, remove the battery and spot clean. Do not machine or hand wash.

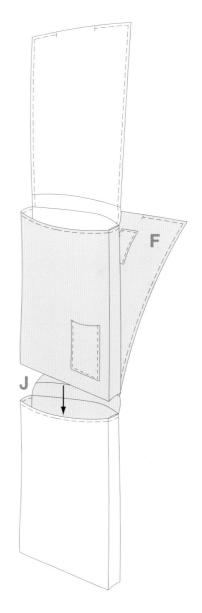

ILLUMINATES WHEN OPENED

Get your clutch out of the dark ages with a purse that shines. As soon as you open the *Shiny Clutch*, a hidden light panel illuminates the interior. No more fumbling and digging for your keys or lip gloss on a night out. Better yet, it also illuminates a personal message on the outside of the purse when open. Express yourself, and let the light shine through.

shiny clutch

[CRAFT] ▣ ▣ ▢   [TECH] ▣ ▣ ▢   [COST] ▣ ▣ ▢

[MATERIALS & TOOLS]

FABRIC A: 1/4 yd (23cm) thin fabric that allows decent amount of light to shine through, such as white leather/pleather or linen

FABRIC B: 1/4 yd (23cm) lightweight fabric

FABRIC C: small piece of sturdy fabric, such as leather or pleather, for handles

Timtex™ interfacing, 2" x 11" (5.1cm x 27.9cm)

5mm thick clear corrugated plastic sheet, 8" x 10" (20.5cm x 25.5cm)

All-purpose thread in a matching color to fabrics A and B

One set of 15mm magnetic purse snaps (1 positive, 1 negative): These are flat (2mm), come in pairs, and each is wrapped in a clear plastic cover.

Six clear LEDs (5mm, high brightness, narrow viewing angle, 3–4 volt)

FABRIC D: 8" x 10" (20.5cm x 25.5cm) black vinyl for the stencil

Cotton batting

Magnetic switch, normally-closed type (page 105)

9-volt battery

Battery snap for 9-volt battery

Optional materials:

White artist tape

Color photo gel, 5 3/4" x 2 1/4" (14.6cm x 5.7cm)

Metal wrist chain, 14" (35.5cm) long

Two fabric grommets, 1/2" (13mm) inside diameter

Core tools (page 106)

PATTERN (page 140)

CUT THE PATTERN

1. Cut out one Body and two Side Panels from fabric A. Cut out one Lining Body, two Side Panels, and one Battery Pocket from fabric B. Cut out two Handles from fabric C. Cut out two Handle Boards from the Timtex. Cut out one Light Panel from the corrugated plastic. .

2. Mark the opening notches on both the Body and Lining Body as marked on the pattern.

MAKE THE HANDLES

3. Using the all-purpose thread, sew the magnetic purse snaps to the Handle Boards. Make sure one button is [+] side up and the other [–] side up.

4. Fold each Handle lengthwise with right sides together and sew the side seams. Clip the corners and turn right side out.

5. Insert one Handle Board into each Handle **(A)**.

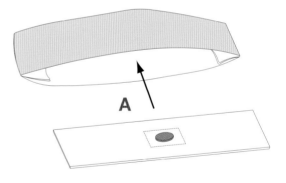

A

✳ **TIP:** If you are using leather, use a 3-ply nylon thread to sew the body and handles. Use rubber cement to glue the seam allowances open on the Side Panels. On step 25, you will not slip stitch. Instead you will press the seam allowance under, leaving the entire notched side open, and then topstitch through all the layers, working from the outside of the bag to finish it.

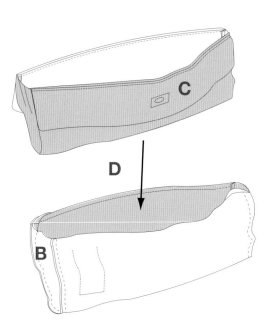

SEW THE LINING

6. Create the buttonhole in the Lining Body as indicated on the pattern.

7. Make the Battery Pocket by turning in the edges ¹⁄₄″ (6mm), and then topstitch the pocket to the Lining Body, as also indicated on the assembly diagram.

8. With right sides together, sew the Lining Side Panels to the Lining Body **(B)**.

MAKE THE BODY

9. With right sides together, sew the Side Panels to the Body.

10. With the magnetic purse snaps pointing out, align and sew the handles to the Body **(C)**.

11. With the Lining wrong side out, insert the Body into the Lining with the handles on the inside of the Lining **(D)**.

12. Align the top edges, sew around the bag, and leave an opening as marked. Now turn the bag right side out.

MAKE THE LIGHT PANEL

13. Insert the LEDs in the corrugated plastic as illustrated below. Note the direction of the **[+]** and **[–]** legs.

14. Bend and overlay two adjacent LED legs, cut off the excess length, and solder them together. Repeat this step with all adjacent legs. You now have two LED chains **(E)**.

15. Follow the diagram carefully: Cut two red 3″ (7.5cm) wires, and solder one to the **[+]** end of each LED chain. Solder the **[+]** wire of the battery holder to one wire of the magnetic switch **(F1)**. Solder the other wire of the switch and the two wires in step F1 together **(F2)**.

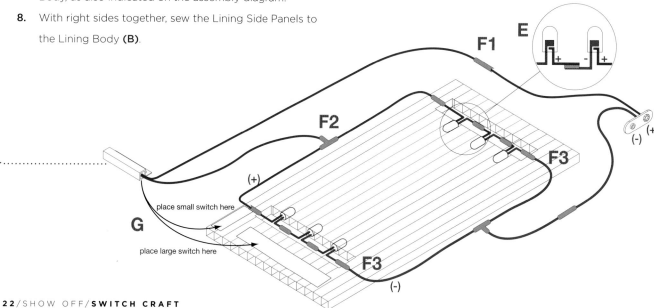

Cut two black 6" (15cm) wires, and solder one to the **[–]** end of each LED chain **(F3)**. Cut one more black 3" (7.5cm wire, solder one end to the **[–]** wire of the battery holder. Solder the other end of the wire and the two wires in step F3 together. Seal all solder joints with hot glue or electrical tape.

16. Glue or tape the wired switch to the Light Panel, its position depending on the size of the switch **(G)**.

17. Cover and seal all edges of the Panel with artist tape or electrical tape.

CREATE YOUR PERSONALIZED TEXT

18. Using an X-Acto® knife and the black vinyl, cut out a stenciled message that will appear on the side of your bag **(H)**. Optional: For a colored message, tape a piece of photo color gel to the back of your cut letters.

19. On the back side of your stencil attach a 6" x 1½" (15cm x 3.8cm) strip of batting at the top.

↺ remix

- What to do if the material or the color that you choose for the clutch is too opaque to let the light through? Try stenciling your message directly on the exterior or punching rows of fine holes in the material.

- If you have an old purse lying around or simply do not want to make your own, try to fit the electronic light panel of the Shiny Clutch into an existing one.

FINISH THE CLUTCH

20. To make the side tucks, fold the side panels in half toward the inside of the bag. Then sew to the edge of the Handle **(I)**.

21. Insert the Light Panel into the Clutch through the opening, keeping the text side facing out **(J)**.

22. Thread the battery clip through the buttonhole and into the Battery Pocket **(K)**.

23. Optional: Secure the Light Panel to the Body using glue to prevent it from moving.

24. Glue the unwired magnetic switch between the Body and Lining. This is directly across from the wired magnetic switch on the Light Panel **(L)**.

25. Slip stitch the opening closed.

> ✳ **TIP: Making It a Wristlet**
> Don't let your Shiny Clutch get away from you. Make it a wristlet by adding grommets and a chain. You can hammer the grommets yourself using a mallet on a hard surface, or have a professional do it at your local fabric notions store. String the chain of your choice through the grommets, and your clutch will never leave your side.

USE & CARE

>> Pull the handles apart to illuminate the interior of the clutch and show off your shiny message.

>> Replace the 9-volt battery when the light grows dim.

>> Do not put credit cards, hard drives, or other magnetically sensitive objects directly next to the magnetic switch and buttons.

>> Spot clean only.

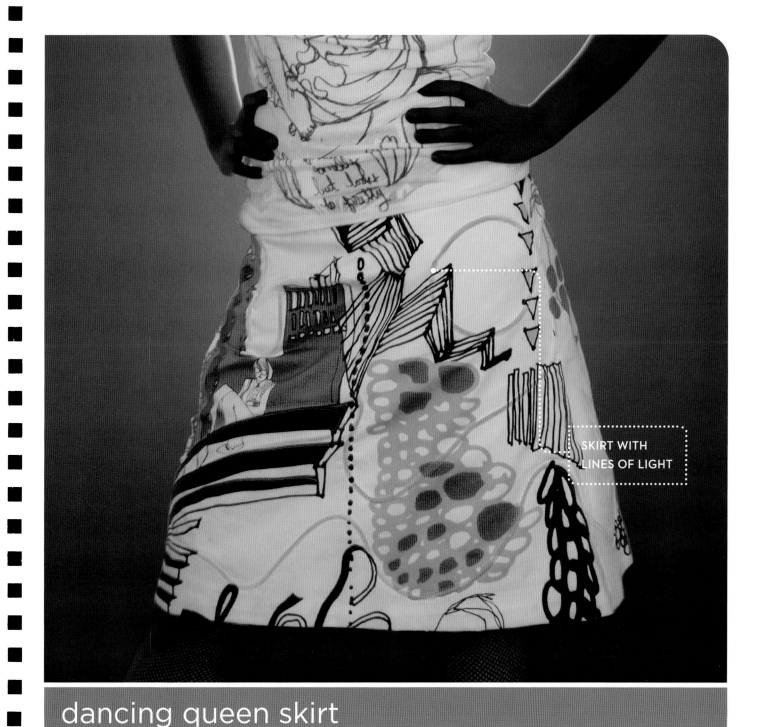

SKIRT WITH
LINES OF LIGHT

dancing queen skirt

Add a little more flair while dancing the night away in the Dancing Queen Skirt. By integrating your fabric skirt with electroluminescent wire, your twists and twirls will leave behind flirtatious trails of light in scintillating color.

dancing queen skirt

[MATERIALS & TOOLS]

Skirt with lining (see step 1 of instructions below)
FABRIC A: 4½" x 4½" (11.4cm x 11.4cm) matching medium-weight fabric
All-purpose thread to match skirt

Portable EL driver (page 106). Pick a small AA battery driver that supports 7' (2.1m) of 3mm EL wire.
7' (2.1m) of 3mm thick EL wire (page 105), in complementary color to your skirt

Core tools (page 106)

✳ **TIP:** Your EL driver often includes a thick molded base to protect the wire from bending. If your driver has this, it is important to include its length when measuring the driver for the patch pocket.

1. Find a skirt you would like to decorate with dazzling light. When choosing a skirt, it is important to find one of a medium- or heavy-weight fabric, such as plain cotton or broadcloth. Choose a skirt made of a light color that will allow the light of the EL wire to shine through. (You can use a darker skirt, but it must have areas of light material or the lights will not shine through.) The skirt cannot have a zipper or other type of opening at the back center—on the side is fine. If you want to make your own skirt instead, we have included a pattern for an A-line side-zip skirt on our website (www.iheartswitch.com/switchcraft).

2. If there is a clip on your EL driver, remove it. Following the instructions on page 109, make a patch pocket for the driver using fabric A.

3. With the skirt inside out, find and mark the center back of your skirt **(A)**. Use a seam ripper to remove the stitches between the skirt exterior and the skirt lining to create an 8" (20.5cm) opening as illustrated **(B)**. Hand-tack the seams at the ends of your opening with 3 to 4 stitches to keep the lining and exterior from separating further **(C)**.

4. Pin and hand-sew the patch pocket into place on the wrong side of the exterior fabric ½" (13mm) away from the edge **(D)**. Turn the skirt right side out.

5. Put the EL driver in the patch pocket, with the wire hanging out **(E)**. Connect the EL wire, and lay it over the right side of the skirt in an aesthetically pleasing design. Once in place, tape the wire down and trace around it, leaving ⅛" (3mm) on each side of the wire, using a fabric-marking pen **(F)**.

6. Using the marked outline as a guide, machine-stitch along the lines, on the right side of the skirt and through the lining, to make a channel for your EL wire.

IMPORTANT: Preventing puckering

To prevent puckering, do the following:

• Use large, smooth curves in your design. The EL wire cannot traverse sharp edges or corners.

• Use a wider stitch (4–6 stitches per inch) to sew the channel.

• Don't rush. Stitch slowly and stop with the needle still in the fabric when making turns.

USE & CARE

>> Turn on the EL driver and light up the town. Twirl and dance to make streams of light.

>> Remove the driver before washing by hand.

>> Make sure the skirt and wire are absolutely dry before reattaching the driver.

>> Change batteries when the light becomes dim.

7. Insert the EL wire into the channel. Watch out for any puckers, and straighten them out as you go. This process may take some time. Be patient! Listen to music or watch TV while you do this.

8. Remove the thread tacks that you sewed earlier at the back of the skirt. Stitch the lining and exterior opening closed. Use the same stitch style as your skirt's original seam, leaving the space above the pocket unstitched so you can add and remove the EL driver.

↻ remix

• Make your own skirt from scratch.

• You may use an EL wire longer than 7' (2.1m) as long as the driver that you choose supports that length.

CUFF WITH SUBTLE,
TASTEFUL GLIMMERS

This charming bracelet catches the eye in an elegant display of beaded light. The Firefly Bracelet is lovely by itself, but when turned on, it transports us to a midsummer night underneath a blanket of stars.

firefly bracelet

[CRAFT] ▢ ▢ ▢   [TECH] ▢ ▢ ▢   [COST] ▢ ▢

[MATERIALS & TOOLS]

FABRIC A, TOP: 4" x 10" (10cm x 25.4cm) wool felt

FABRIC B, BOTTOM: 4" X 10" (10cm x 25.4cm) wool felt

Variety of accent felt squares in colors of your choice

Two LED Beads (page 120)

Quick-Change Skinny Power Pack (page 115); uses five size-10 hearing aid batteries

Magnetic clasps, as suggested in the Power Pack materials on page 115

Conductive thread (page 104)

All-purpose thread to match fabric A

Variety of transparent glass, crystal, or acrylic beads for decoration around the LED lights; we used five to seven 4–6mm multicolored glass and crystal beads for each LED flower.

4 small red beads (3 or 4mm)

4 small black beads (3 or 4mm)

EMBELLISHMENTS: embroidery thread, beads, and adornments of your choice

Superfine micro round-nose pliers

Beading needle

Beading wire

Two small magnets, 1/4" (6mm), two for the battery pack, two for the switch. We used ProMag button magnets.

Reed switch (page 105)

One pair of sew-on snaps (size 2/0)

Bracelet base, adjustable cuff style

Core tools (page 106)

PATTERN (page 128)

PREPARE THE PATTERN

1. From the patterns, cut one Bracelet Top from fabric A, one Bracelet Bottom from fabric B, and four Large Circles plus one Small Circle from the accent fabric squares.

2. Make two LED Beads according to the instructions on page 120. Also make a Quick-Change Skinny Power Pack using five hearing aid batteries (page 115); do not put in the magnetic clasps yet.

MAKE THE LED FLOWERS

3. Center one LED Bead on a Large Circle. Using two separate conductive threads, stitch the [+] and [–] sides of the Bead to the Fabric **(A)**. Loop each thread through the hole on the Bead's [+] or [–] leg several times to fasten before knotting it underneath. Leave at least 4" (10cm) hanging at the end for each thread. Seal the knots with a tiny dab of hot glue on the wrong side. Mark the [+] and [–] on the wrong side using a felt-tip pen. Now sew several translucent beads onto the Circle to cover the LED Bead **(B)**.

4. Repeat the previous step on another Large Circle to make the second LED Flower.

5. Sew the LED Flowers onto the right side of the Bracelet Top as marked on the pattern. Pull each conductive thread through to the wrong side and tie off with a small black bead for the [–] thread and a small red bead for the [+] thread **(C)**. Do not snip the threads yet.

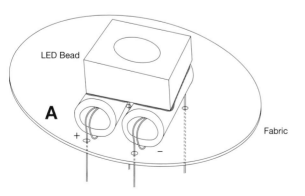

↻ remix

- Design a necklace or other accessory to go along with your cuff.
- If you'd like to add more LEDs, keep in mind that for every additional LED, you need two more hearing aid batteries.

TIP: To make sure the beads diffuse the light and make a soft glow, connect your [+] and [-] threads to a 3-volt battery (page 102) to turn the LED on, and adjust the beads.

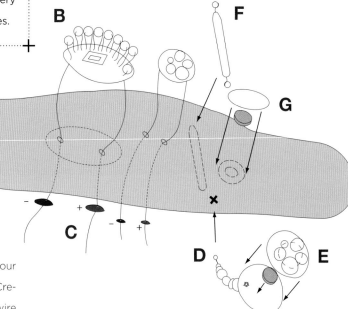

CREATE THE SWITCH

6. Take a 3" (7.5cm) piece of beading wire and string your favorite beads, leaving about ½" (13mm) on each end. Create a loop at both ends of the wire and tuck the extra wire from the loop under the closest bead. Twist the wire to secure **(D)**. Sew one loop to a Large Circle as illustrated and sew the other loop to the right side of the Bracelet Top where marked.

7. Create another cluster of beads, like you did in step 3, and sew them onto a Large Circle. It should look just like your LED Flowers, but without the LED Bead **(E)**. Sandwich a magnet between the beaded circle and the wired circle, and sew ⅛" around the edges. This is the activator for your switch.

8. To make the other part of the switch, you'll need to sew on the reed switch. Use the round-nose pliers to gently curl each end of the reed switch into a loop—be careful, because the wires can be fragile **(F)**. With one 4" (10cm) conductive thread for each loop, sew the switch to the right side of the Bracelet Top as marked. Be sure to loop each thread through the switch's loop 4 to 5 times before knotting to ensure good electrical conductivity. Don't snip the excess threads. Let them hang from the wrong side.

9. Attach the other magnet onto the Bracelet Top by sewing the Small Circle over it. This is your activator base **(G)**. Make sure it attracts, not repels, the activator, otherwise you will need to flip the magnet over.

COMPLETE THE CIRCUIT

10. Flip the Bracelet Top to the wrong side. Following the diagram, tie the [+] thread of LED Flower 1 with the [-] thread of LED Flower 2. Make sure the knot is tight and the thread is taut, but doesn't pull the fabric **(H)**. Tie the [+] thread of Flower 2 with the bottom thread of the reed switch. Knot and pull tightly **(I)**. Now hot-glue the start and end points of these two tied threads, cut off any excess, and cover both threads with electrical tape.

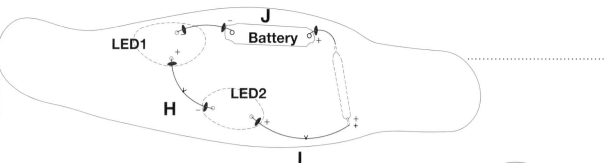

11. Securely knot the [–] thread of Flower 1 around the hoop of a magnetic clasp, tie off with a small black bead, and secure both ends with hot glue. Do the same to the top thread of the switch and the other clasp but use a small red bead to indicate that it is the [+] side.

12. Place your Battery Pack on the mark and secure it with electrical tape. Insert the magnetic clasps into the Pack, being mindful that the [+] and the [–] of the battery and the clasps match up (J). Cover these two last threads with electrical tape.

13. The circuit is completed. Test the circuit by moving your activator (with the magnet) from the activator base over to the reed switch. This should turn on the LEDs.

PUT IT ALL TOGETHER

14. Decorate the rest of your bracelet to your liking. We used lots of beads and fabric shapes in random patterns. Sew on the snaps to the wrong side of the Bracelet Top and to the right side of the Bracelet Bottom as marked.

15. Center and hot-glue the Bracelet Top to the bracelet base. Sew the Top and Bottom together with the bracelet base sandwiched between (K).

USE & CARE

>> Place the Switch Activator on the reed switch to turn on the LEDs. To turn off, place it on its magnetic base.

>> Spot clean only.

>> Replace the battery pack when needed.

>> Keep the magnets away from things that are magnetically sensitive, such as credit cards or hard drives.

Chapter Two: Share Alike

Don't keep it all to yourself; spread the love.

FABRIC CHARM
WITH RECORDER

With its ornate and luxe design, this monogrammed charm contains an audio recorder to offer a stylish way to pour your heart out without missing a beat. It's small enough to be packed into luggage for that long trip apart, and convenient enough to leave in a bag for an unexpected hello. Use it to tell friends where you are going and what you're doing or record your inspiration at the spur of the moment.

whisper charm

[MATERIALS & TOOLS]

Keychain audio recorder (see sidebar at right)

Iron-on transfer paper

FABRIC A, EXTERIOR: ¼ yd (23cm) medium-
 weight brocade or metallic fabric

¼" (6mm) iron-on batting

THREAD A: all-purpose thread

THREAD B: embroidery thread, metallic color
 recommended

Embroidery needle

6" (15cm) ribbon, of complementary color to
 Fabric A

Snap closure, Size 3/0

Two different-sized buttons of your choice to
 match the design

Jewels, chains, and small charms of your choice

Core tools (page 106)

KEYCHAIN AUDIO RECORDER

You should be able to find a cheap recorder keychain on websites like eBay or Amazon, online electronics stores, or brick-and-mortar stores like Bed, Bath and Beyond. Don't be distracted by bells and whistles (like a built-in alarm clock); look for recorders that are small and thin and have separate buttons for recording and playback. Stay away from overpriced models sold on TV infomercials and ones with tiny recessed buttons that can only be operated with a pin.

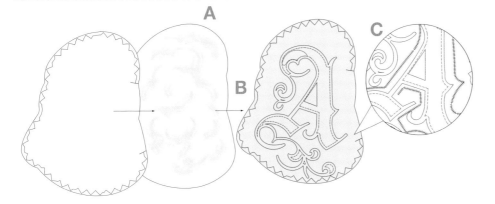

CUT THE PATTERN

1. Remove any chains, key rings, or other extras attached to your keychain recorder.

2. Measure the height and width of the recorder. On your computer, in a word processing or drawing program, enlarge a letter in a font of your choosing and print it onto an iron-on transfer sheet, following the manufacturer's directions. We used a font called BlackLetter, but a similar font will work.**3.** Staying as close to the image edge as possible, cut out the monogram with an X-Acto knife and lay it on your fabric.

Transfer the image following the directions on the package With a fabric pen, draw a smooth, flowing line around the monogram in an aesthetically pleasing way. Make sure the line is at least ½" (13mm) away from the image edge.

4. Measure and mark a line ½" (13mm) out from the line you just drew for the seam allowance, and cut the shape out. This will be the Monogram Front.

5. Cut two more pieces of fabric in an identical shape to the monogrammed piece from fabric A. Place one aside for now, and iron the quilted batting on to the wrong side of the other piece **(A)**.

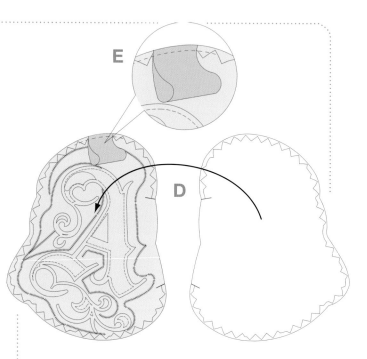

TIP: Iron-on transfer paper is made for cotton T-shirts and requires a high temperature to melt the adhesives. If you are using synthetic fabrics that scorch easily, place a sheet of muslin or scrap of cotton between the fabric and the iron.

6. To quilt the Monogram Front, place the back piece you just created and the Monogram Front with right sides together **(B)**. Sew a ¼" (6mm) zigzag stitch around the edges, leaving an opening large enough to turn right side out. Use a blunt edge (such as a pen tip) to turn the tight corners, curves, and angles fully out.

7. Fold under the unfinished edges, pin, and slipstitch shut.

8. Embellish the front with topstitching by accentuating the shape of the monogram with a contrasting metallic thread **(C)**.

9. Cut away ¼" (6mm) from around the other piece of fabric that you set aside in step 5. Now pin the trimmed piece, right sides together, to the quilted Monogram Top piece **(D)**. Fold the matching ribbon in half with right sides together. Pin the bottom edges of your ribbon between the two layers at the top of the Whisper Charm. Sew a ¼" (6mm) seam around the Charm, leaving an opening large enough for your recorder to be easily inserted and removed **(E)**. Turn right side out.

10. Hand-sew around the edges of your Whisper Charm with a unique stitch, such as whipstitch, with your accent thread.

11. Finish the opening by folding under the edges and sewing around the flaps with the same decorative stitch. Hand-sew on a snap closure to the top and bottom **(F)**.

USE & CARE

>> Push the record button to store a message, and the play button to hear it again.

>> When the battery is low, open the Charm and take out the recorder. Refer to its manual for instructions regarding battery replacement.

TIP: If you don't want to use a whipstitch like we did, look at the variety of stitches on your sewing machine for inspiration. Try out a couple of stitch types on a sample piece of fabric and pick one you like for the edges of the Charm.

12. Fit the recorder inside the finished pocket and snap it closed. Mark the location of the recording and playback button switches with a fabric pen. Sew on the fabric buttons directly over the location of the player buttons **(G)**.

13. Test your buttons to ensure they trigger the recording and the playback. Finish them by adding decorative stitches. We used long and short gold stitches to make the play button look like a star and only simple stitching on the record button. This further distinguishes these two buttons visually.

14. Finish off your Whisper Charm by adding ribbons, jewels, and other small charms that complement your design.

TIP: We push play more than record, therefore the play button should be a larger and more distinct button. Also, the tactile feedback of different sizes will help you to operate the Charm without having to look.

from edison's phonograph to the female workforce

When Edison unveiled his phonograph in 1877, few—if any—could foresee this sound recording device playing an intimate role in the empowerment of women. In the late nineteenth and early twentieth century, there was an explosion of office technology inventions. Among them, the phonograph and typewriter were closely linked to the rise of the female workforce. According to Angel Kwolek-Folland, the percentage of stenographers and typists who were women skyrocketed from 5% in 1870 to 96% in 1930. Together with their bookkeeping, accounting, and other clerical sisters, they took over the majority of clerical positions (53%) in 1930. An impressive feat, considering that the number was 2.5% back in 1870. So next time you see one of those turn-of-the-century photos depicting a female stenographer transcribing her male boss' comments, do not carelessly dismiss it as an archaic prctice. She was a proud pioneer who blazed the way for womankind.

G

F

↻ remix

- Instead of ironing on the monogram, appliqué it to create a more distinctive look.
- Think of other techniques, such as quilting, to make the Charm even more three-dimensional.
- Change the design style of Whisper Charm to fit your outfits.

FRIDGE MAGNET
REMINDER

petit four d-light

Petit Four D-Lights are delicious-looking petite magnets for those sweet little messages. Just toggle the switch, and these non-edible treats light up. Best of all, these eye candies are nonfattening!

[CRAFT] ■ ▦ ▦   [TECH] ■ ▦ ▦   [COST] ■ ▦ ▦

[MATERIALS & TOOLS]

FABRIC A, EXTERIOR: 4" x 4" (10cm x 10cm) square of thin jersey knit
4" x 4" (10cm x 10cm) square of iron-on batting
All-purpose thread to match Fabric A
1/4" (6mm) wide elastic
Clear acrylic box with lid, 1" x 1" x 3/4" (2.5cm x 2.5cm x 2cm)

EMBELLISHMENTS: ribbons, embroidery thread, or beads of your choice. We used 1/8" (3mm) silk ribbon and six long silver beads for the corset design.
SPST slide switch (page 105)
3 wires each 1/2" (13mm) long
Secure Skinny Power Pack (page 115) that uses two size-10 hearing aid batteries

LED Button (page 117). 3mm LED, color of your choice. Two-hole button, about 3/4" (2cm) wide
1 1/4" (3cm) foil candy cup
One button magnet
Utility knife or acrylic cutter
Core tools (page 106)
PATTERN (page 133)

1. Cut out one Petit Four Body from fabric A and batting. Cut the elastic to 4" (10 cm). Iron on the batting Body to the wrong side of fabric A Body. Machine or hand-stitch the buttonhole, leaving it closed for now **(A)**.

2. With right sides together, fold and dart three of the four corners. Trim to 1/8" (3mm) and press open. On the wrong side, zigzag stitch the elastic around the perimeter of the bottom edges of the Body.

3. Sew the last corner and clip and press open. Use an X-Acto knife to slice open the buttonhole. Embellish the top with ribbon, beads, or stitches to your liking **(B)**.

4. To prepare your plastic box so it fits your electronics, you will need to make a hole for the switch. Measure the width and height of the switch body (the part behind the mounting ears, see page 105). The hole will need to be the same size as the body of your switch and will be cut in the center, flush against the upper edge of one side of the box body. Use your utility knife or acrylic cutter to cut the opening, starting at the top edge and working down toward the bottom using a delicate sawing motion **(C)**.

5. Then cut a hole the same width as the hole you just made in the lid of the box on one side of the lid. When the box is closed, the two holes should line up.

6. Cut three 1 1/2" (3.8cm) long wires (we suggest using three different colors). Use two of these and two size-10 hearing aid batteries to make a Secure Skinny Power Pack according to page 116 **(D)**. Follow the instructions on page 117 to make an LED Button with one 3mm LED **(E)**.

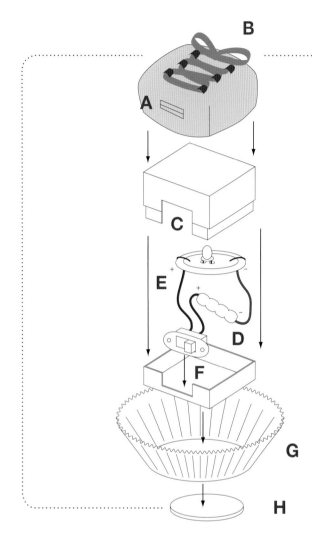

7. Solder the [−] wire from the Skinny Power Pack to the [−] leg of the LED Button, and the [+] wire to one terminal of the switch. Now solder the remaining wire to the other terminal and the [+] leg of the LED Button.

8. Cover the bottom of the LED button with electrical tape. Insulate the switch terminals with electrical tape or hot glue.

9. Place the switch into the hole on the box lid. The body of the switch should sit inside the box and the mounting ears outside **(F)**. Now, fit the Skinny Power Pack and the LED into the Box. The LED lamp needs to shine out of the bottom of the box, and the battery fits best in the lid. This is a very tight space, and it may take several attempts to fit all of the items into your box. Once you have fit everything and can close the box, seal it with invisible tape and secure the mounting ears of your switch. Do not tape over the part of the switch that needs to slide.

10. Glue the foil candy cup to the bottom of the box **(G)**, and glue the magnet to the bottom of the candy cup **(H)**. Insert the box into the Petit Four Body, and put the switch toggle through the buttonhole.

11. Get creative and make as many as you want, using fabulous and fun embellishments.

USE & CARE

>> Stick the Petit Four on your refrigerator and use it as a regular fridge magnet.

>> Turn on the LED to bring people's attention to a special or important note.

>> Try putting multiple petit fours in a real candy box. It looks great and makes a unique gift.

>> Keep the magnet away from things that are magnetically sensitive, such as credit cards or hard drives.

↻ remix

- Think of all the different kinds of candies and cakes you love to eat, and try to mimic them with ribbons, beads, or embroidery.
- If you'd like to use a blinking LED or color-changing LED, you may need a bigger acrylic box. Enlarge the pattern accordingly.
- Paint the switch with acrylic paint or nail polish in a color that goes with your design.

let there be light

Today, the electric light is just another mundane daily object, and it's easy to forget how awe-inspiring this invention once was. A reporter in 1899 marveled at the newly installed lights in Omaha:

[Above the city] will hang a misty cloud of light, playing on the heavens and shaming into shadow the twinkling stars. Viewed from a distance it might be mistaken for the light from a terrible conflagration but that it shines so clear and has no pall or pillar of dark smoke to mar its radiance.

Of course people soon wanted to show off the new wonder in creative ways. See the "electric jewelry" from Paris (1888): *Electric jewelry usually takes the form of pins, which are made in various designs. One such trifle copies a daisy, and has an electric spark flash-ing from the center, another is a model of a lantern in emerald glass, while a death's head in gold, with a ray gleaming from each eye, is a third.*

And behold Marquisse de Belbeuf's custom dress (1884): *It is her fancy to enter a ball-room crowned with a wreath of autumn blossoms, not too bright in colors, and with a bouquet of similar flowers in her corsage. Presently she touches a secret spring and both wreath and bouquet are brilliant with electric light.* Now that's bling!

INTIMATE MOBILE
PHONE HEADSET

pillow talk

We know how much you enjoy those late-night chats. Ever fall asleep on the phone, only to wake up with a crook in your neck, or even worse, wake up with the phone's impression on your cheek? Hook up your mobile phone to Pillow Talk and cozy up for all your wee hour gossips or sweet nothings.

[CRAFT] ▪ ▪ □   [TECH] ▪ ▪ ▪   [COST] ▪ ▪ □

[MATERIALS & TOOLS]

FABRIC A, PILLOW FABRIC: 1 yd (0.9m) anything soft; we used a cashmere/cotton blend with a fuzzy texture.

FABRIC B, FABRIC STRIPS FOR POM POM: 1/3 yd (30.5cm) jersey knit in contrasting color; use your boyfriend's old T-shirt.

THREAD A, ACCENT: 100% polyester embroidery floss in a color 4 shades lighter than fabric A

THREAD B, STITCHING: all-purpose cotton/poly thread to match fabric A

Embroidery needle

Sticky labels

Plastic canvas sheet, #7 mesh, 13 1/2" x 10 1/2" (34.5cm x 26.5cm)

Mobile phone headset with answer/end button (see below)

Donut Switch (page 119). Use a 7 1/2" x 5 1/4" (19cm x 13.2cm) grout sponge.

Cotton stuffing

Core tools (page 106)

PATTERN (page 134)

MOBILE-PHONE HEADSET

To make Pillow Talk, you'll be opening up your headset cord, then taking what is inside and connecting it somewhere else. It's not brain surgery, so if you make a mistake don't worry about it. Nobody's life is at risk here—well, except maybe for your headset's! Luckily, they can be inexpensive. Our advice is simple: Buy the cheapest headset that is compatible with your cell phone. eBay and your local discount stores are good places to look for deals. Although it doesn't matter if the headset has one or two earbuds, there must be a microphone unit on it with a built-in answer/end button. Do not purchase a wireless headset.

MAKE THE PILLOW

1. Mark and cut two Pillow Body pieces from fabric A. From fabric B, cut out 65 3/4" (1.7m) wide by 6" (15cm) long strips.

2. Pick one Body piece to be the Body Front and cut out the circle as shown in the pattern, then hand-stitch two rows of long basting stitches (approximately 1/2" [1.25cm] apart) around the circle, leaving about 4" (10cm) of thread hanging at the end of each row. Pull the excess thread to decrease the opening of the circle to 3 1/2" (9 cm) in diameter **(A)**. Arrange the gathers around your circle evenly. Cut and knot the threads.

3. Using the embroidery floss, embroider a straight stitch along the line marked on the pattern, starting below the circle **(B)**.

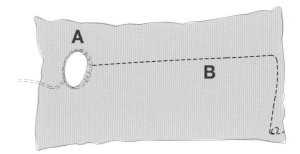

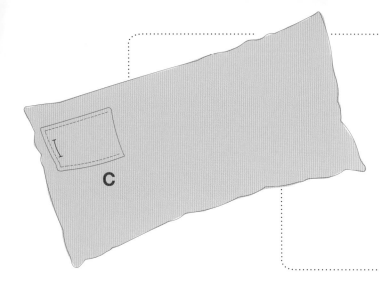

C

OPEN THE HEADSET

9. Take a good look at the headset cable between the micro-phone unit and headset jack. Look to see if yours is made with a single wire or two wires bonded side by side. If you have a single wire, skip this step. If you have a double wire, use an X-Acto knife to slice a 3″ (7.5cm) opening between the bonded wires, midway between the microphone unit and the headset jack **(F)**.

> ✳ **TIP:** Don't worry if your headset looks different from the illustration. As long as it contains one or two earbuds and one microphone unit with a built-in answer/end button, you are fine.

4. Using the back Body piece, create a buttonhole as marked on the pattern. Now create a patch pocket (page 109) that fits your mobile phone with a 1/2″ (13mm) seam allowance. Align the Phone Pocket to the bottom edge as marked, and center it over the buttonhole as best you can **(C)**.

5. With right sides together, sew the Body Front and Body Back together, leaving an opening as marked. Turn right side out.

10. If your headset cable is of a single wire, cut away a 2″ (5cm) segment of the plastic coating from the wire, midway be-tween the microphone unit and the headset jack. If yours is a double wire, do the same to both wires that you separated in the last step. After removing the coat you should see ei-ther three or four inner wires **(G)**. If you see three wires, skip the following instructions pertaining to W4. If you see only two, they may be coaxial cables, each consisting of 2 inner wires—please refer to page 103 to see how to separate wires from a coaxial cable.

CREATE THE POM-POM

6. Cut the plastic canvas sheet to be exactly 1/2″ (13mm) in di-ameter larger than the circular hole in the Pillow.

7. Fold the strips in half and tie each one, leaving a knot in the middle. Starting from the center of the plastic canvas, thread one end of a knotted strip through a hole in the plastic can-vas. Thread the other end through an adjacent hole. Pull the strip tightly so the knot is flush with the plastic canvas **(D)**. Continue until the canvas is filled with fabric strips, leaving a 1/2″ (13mm) border empty **(E)**.

8. Hand-sew the plastic sheet behind the Pillow opening, Pom-Pom facing front. Fluff, clip, and manipulate the fabric strips as desired.

> ✳ **TIP:** If you want your strips to be extra secure, sew them to the plastic mesh.

D

E

11. The inner wires most likely will be coated with colored plastic insulation. If they are not color-coded, mark the wires W1, W2, W3, and W4 using sticky labels. If your wires are not covered in plastic, but are still color-coated, then you most likely have magnet wires—please refer to page 103 for more information.

12. Snip the wires at their center points. If these wires have plastic coating, carefully strip away ¹/₂″ (13mm) from the cut. If these are magnet wires (refer to page 102), use a nail file to scratch away the insulation layer ¹/₂″ (13mm) from the cut **(H)**.

13. Now you will have to do some detective work. Find out which two wires when connected can answer or hang up a call. Do this by plugging the headset jack to your phone. Use another phone to call yourself and wait until the phone rings. When your cell phone is ringing, connect one wire to another wire (hold it for 3 seconds and release) to see if the call is picked up. For example, touch wire W1 to W2. If the call is answered, try connecting the wires again to see if the call is terminated. Follow the Testing Table on page 46 to test different wire combinations until you find the combination of two wires that does the job.

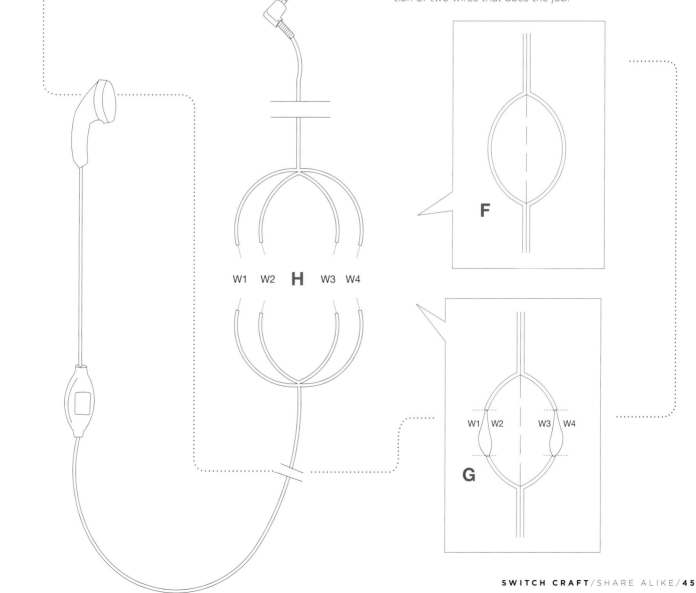

W1   W2   **H**   W3   W4

F

W1 W2   W3 W4

G

TESTING TABLE

	Works? (Y/N)
W1 + W2	Y/N
W1 + W3	Y/N
W1 + W4	Y/N
W2 + W3	Y/N
W2 + W4	Y/N
W3 + W4	Y/N

14. Cut two 20″ (51cm) wires and label them D1 and D2. Solder the two ends of W1, W2, W3, and W4 back together. You also need to solder D1 and D2 to the wires that you discovered in the previous step. We use W3 and W4 as an example in the illustration, but yours may be different **(I)**. Secure all solder joints with hot glue.

15. Prepare your Donut Switch for the pillow by slicing the grout sponge diagonally to make a large triangle. Cut two pieces of conductive fabric in the same shape as the sponge and follow the directions on page 119, using D1 and D2 wires for connection to the switch's wires. Solder D1 to one switch wire and solder D2 to the other wire and cover the connections with electrical tape **(J)**.

↺ remix

- If the headset hacking seems too complicated, you may make a pillow without the switch and simply insert your headset without hacking. While you can still talk using the pillow, you must use your phone to answer or terminate calls.
- Cut the earbud and replace it with a small, self-powered portable speaker. This will make your pillow a speakerphone.

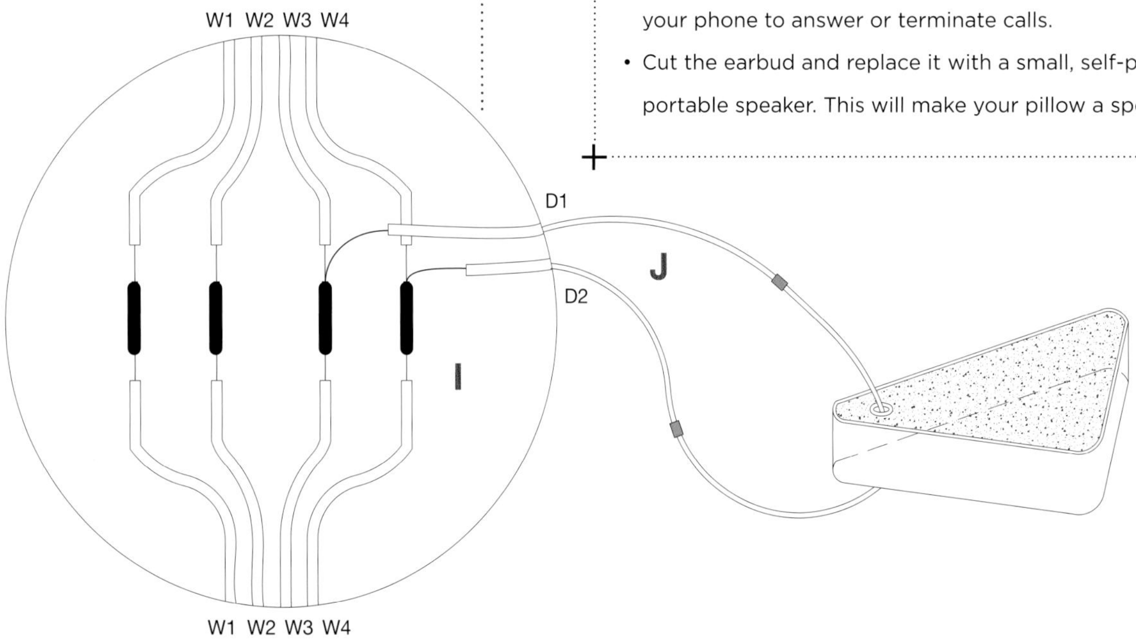

W1 W2 W3 W4

D1

D2

J

I

W1 W2 W3 W4

PUT THEM TOGETHER

16. Insert the Donut Switch into the corner under the square-shaped embroidery, and slipstitch it to the seam allowance to keep it in place. Place the earbud(s) under the center of the Pom-Pom and the microphone unit about 4″ (10 cm) and 45 degrees down from the earbud(s). Hand-sew them to the plastic canvas sheet. Pull the headset jack through the buttonhole into the Phone Pocket **(K)**.

17. Being mindful of the electronics, stuff the pillow to desired firmness, test the phone and switch again, and then slipstitch the pillow closed.

USE & CARE

>> To answer a call, squeeze the corner where the donut switch is located for about 3 seconds and release. Do the same to hang up.

>> Lay your head down on the soft Pom-Pom to talk.

>> Wash with a washcloth and appropriate cleaning solution.

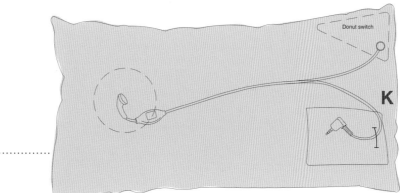

Donut switch

K

party lines and pillow talk

As cell phones assimilate more and more into our daily lives, they are fast becoming personal mp3 players, cameras, and even portable computers. This makes it very difficult to imagine that only fifty years ago people shared their phone lines with someone from their neighborhood or even perfect strangers. Before WWII, party lines were popular in the United States and England. People would save money by sharing the same phone line with other families. Instead of their own private line, each household sharing the line would have their own distinctive ring. For nosy neighbors, this was a treasure: If the phone was already in use you could eavesdrop on your shared parties' conversations.

Pillow Talk also got its inspiration from the 1959 Academy Award-winning film starring Rock Hudson and Doris Day. *Pillow Talk* follows the comedic pitfalls of eavesdropping and party lines, and the strange and romantic things that can happen from sharing a communication channel.

KISS AND LIGHT UP KEYCHAIN CREATURES

Celebrate your inner child or brighten someone else's with two modern, handmade companions that light up when they kiss. Is that how someone in your life makes you feel? Show them with Lovie Circuits.

lovie circuits

[CRAFT]    [TECH]   [COST] ▪

[MATERIALS & TOOLS]

FABRIC A, BODY: ¼ yd (23cm) of nonwoven fabric, such as suede or wool felt

FABRIC B, HEART: 8" x 8" (20.5cm x 20.5cm) lightweight white cotton fabric

All-purpose thread to match fabric A

Two jewelry or keychain clasps

Two 6" (15cm) strips of ½" (13mm) ribbon in complementary color to your fabrics

Conductive thread (page 104)

Two Battery Snap Caps (page 116)

Two pairs of sew-on snaps (size 1/0)

Two LED Buttons with Reflective Cones (page 117). We used red 5mm flashing LEDs, 3–4 volt.

One set of 15mm magnetic buttons.

Cotton stuffing

Core tools (page 106)

PATTERN (page 139)

CUT THE PATTERN

1. Cut one Lovie Body A, one Lovie Body B, two Lovie Sides (without the heart), and one Battery Pocket from fabric A. Cut one Magnet Holder and one Heart from fabric B.

> **TIP:** If you want to make a really fat Lovie, you can cut the Body pieces on the bias.

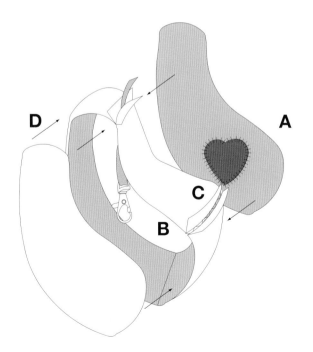

MAKE THE BODY

2. Cut out a heart-shaped hole from only one of the two Side pieces. Sew the Heart Background to the back side of the heart-shaped hole with a buttonhole stitch around the edges of the heart **(A)**.

3. Slip the keychain clasp onto your ribbon, and fold the ribbon in half. Pin the folded ribbon between Body A and Body B at the dot and sew a ⅛" (3mm) seam to make the Body **(B)**.

4. Baste stitch the raw edges of the Body together with a ⅛" (3mm) seam allowance. Fold open and iron flat **(C)**.

5. With right sides together, sew both Sides of the Lovie together, leaving about a 1½" (3.8cm) opening at one side of the neck **(D)**.

> **TIP:** Practice making your buttonhole stitch (which is a really tight zigzag stitch) with a high stitches-per-inch setting on your sewing machine. Try different widths and settings on scrap fabric before stitching the heart. If you don't like the zigzag stitch, you can use sewing glue to seal the edges and do a simple straight stitch about ⅛" (3mm) away from the heart hole, stitching it all the way around.

IMPORTANT: Smooth side seams

To ensure a good seam, sew the side pieces onto the Lovie like you would a sleeve, into an armhole on a shirt. Make a wide baste stitch, and pull the thread to align the two sides together before sewing the final stitch. At this stage it is also recommended that you turn the Lovie right side out through the opening, inspect it for any wrinkles or sewing errors, and make adjustments.

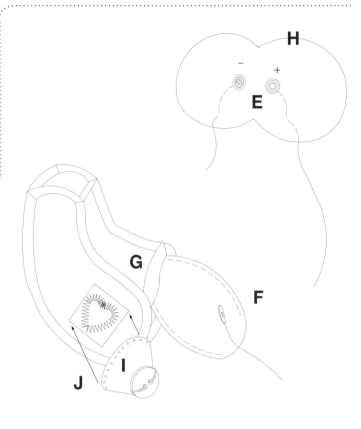

CREATE THE BATTERY POCKET

6. Following the directions on page 110, prepare two gripper snap prong rings with two different pieces of conductive thread, one at least 12″ (30.5cm) long and another at least 30″ (76cm) long.

7. Attach gripper snaps to the marked circles on the Battery Pocket, with the shorter thread attached to the stud gripper snap, and the longer thread attached to the socket gripper snap **(E)**.

8. Fold the Pocket with right sides facing (the threads should be on the outside), and sew the sides of the Pocket up to the circle marks **(F)**. Finish by stitching the sew-on snaps with the all-purpose thread to the top curve of the Pocket. With the Pocket still inside out, pin and sew it to the basted ⅛″ (3mm) seam of the body **(G)**.

9. Remove the basted stitches you created in step 4, and iron the seams flat. Pull the threads on the back prongs of the gripper snaps in opposite directions, and then use fabric glue or a small bit of hot glue to secure the conductive threads to the back of the gripper snaps.

10. Mark a [−] next to the gripper snap with the 12″ (30.5cm) thread and mark a [+] next to the gripper snap with the 30″ (76cm) thread with a permanent marker **(H)**.

11. Create your Battery Snap Cap from page 116. Test to make sure it snaps in and out of your battery pocket, and test conductivity with your multimeter (page 108).

IMPORTANT: For the following steps, please refer to the diagrams on opposite page. Be sure to read the warning information.

SEW THE CIRCUIT

12. Create an LED Button with one LED and a reflective cone (page 117). Poke small holes into the LED reflective cone with a needle or pin, about ⅛″ (3mm) from the edge **(I)**. With the cone facing the wrong side of the heart shape (so the LED will shine through the heart) and the side of the LED facing toward the [−] battery snap, use the cone holes you just made to sew the cone to the back of the Heart fabric **(J)**.

13. Take the thread from the [−] marked gripper snap and wrap it around the [−] marked wire of your LED Button 3 to 4 times until secure, leaving a small amount of slack. Tie a knot and cut off any excess thread **(K)**.

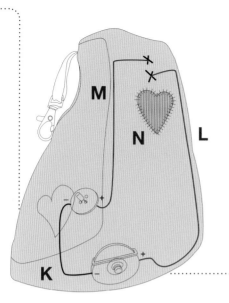

TIP: The magnet will pull your needle and make it difficult to sew the top shut. The best thing to do is work slowly and be patient when stitching.

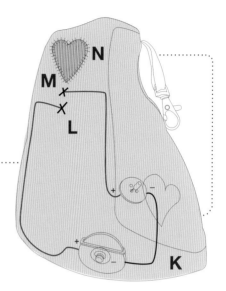

14. Take the thread from the **[+]** marked gripper snap and sew it up the inside seam allowance. Then use the thread to create the bottom embroidered X **(L)**. Leave enough slack so that it doesn't pull the seam and distort the shape of the Lovie. Cut off the excess thread, and secure it with fabric glue.

15. Using a new piece of thread, about 14" (35.5) long, sew the upper embroidered X on the face, and then sew the excess down the empty seam opposite the one you sewed down earlier **(M)**. Wrap the thread around the **[+]** marked wire of your LED Button 3 to 4 times. Tie a knot, cut the excess, and insulate the back of the LED button with hot glue.

 CAUTION: Before hot gluing, make sure the [+] and [–] threads are not crossed or touching anywhere in the Lovie.

16. Embroider the heart shape on the Lovie's face with a new piece of conductive thread, using long straight stitches. Knot, cut away excess, and secure with fabric glue **(N)**.

17. Test the two embroidered Xs with your multimeter to make sure there is no connection between them (page 108).

↺ remix

- Enlarge the Lovies if you want them to be huggable.
- Experiment with colors and textures. Spice it up further by adding ornaments or eye-catching stitches.
- Remove the magnetic buttons to reduce the Lovies' urge to kiss!

ADD THE MAGNET

18. Turn the Lovie inside out, if it's not already. Keeping the magnet inside its plastic sleeve with the right side facing out, position the magnet as marked. Secure the magnet by sewing each side of the magnet sleeve to the inside seams with a zigzag stitch.

19. Turn the Lovie right side out. Snap the 3-volt Battery Holder into the Battery Pocket. Insert the battery, making sure that the [+] and [–] of the battery matches the [+] and [–] sides of the holder and gripper snaps.

20. Test by placing a straight pin over both embroidered Xs simultaneously; the magnet should hold it in place. This action should turn on your LED. If this does not happen, read through the instructions again carefully. Ensure that all threads are separate and the battery is installed correctly.

PUT THEM TOGETHER

21. After testing, remove the straight pin and stuff the Lovie. Spread the stuffing evenly so that your Lovie can sit up on its own. Slipstitch the opening closed.

22. Make the second Lovie. This time cut the heart-shaped hole on the opposite Side piece of the Lovie, making them mirror images of each other. Also reverse the order of the embroidered Xs and the heart, as seen on the diagram, page 51. Test to ensure the magnets are attracting properly before inserting a magnet into the second doll.

USE & CARE

>> Hold the Lovies together, both facing each other, and watch them express their affections with beautiful light-up hearts.

>> Replace the battery when needed.

>> Spot clean only.

>> Keep credit cards, hard drives, and other magnetically sensitive objects away from the magnets.

TOTE WITH REMOVABLE SPEAKERS

urban blaster

How many times have you been at the park, beach, or just hanging out and wanted to create an instant party? This tote has removable snap-in/snap-out speakers. Simply plug in your MP3 player and share your music with a special few or a crowd wherever you happen to go. Talk about causing a scene!

urban blaster

[CRAFT] ■ ■ ■   [TECH] ■ ■ ■   [COST] ■ ■ ■

[MATERIALS & TOOLS]

FABRIC A, EXTERIOR: 2½ yd (1.4m) heavyweight or lightweight cotton, denim, or barkcloth. Extra yardage is needed for matching or centering a pattern on fabric. We used "Inked Attitude," a lightweight cotton print from Alexander Henry.

FABRIC B, BUCKET: ⅓ yd (30.5cm) coated nylon

Fabric C, LINING: 2 yd (1.8m) coated nylon. We used the same coated nylon for the Lining and the Bucket.

All-purpose thread in a matching color to fabric A

INTERFACING: ¼ yd medium-weight iron-on interfacing or 2¾ yd (2.5m) of interfacing if you are using a lightweight cotton exterior fabric

⅓ yd (30.5cm) Timtex™ interfacing. If you do not have Timtex, use a heavy-duty interfacing for the Bucket and cardboard for the Dividers.

Fold-up Speaker Set (see sidebar at right)

Zipper foot

16" (40.5cm) zipper in coordinating color to Fabric B. We used a waterproof zipper.

FABRIC D, SPEAKER COVER: 4" x 4" (10cm x 10cm) nylon mesh square

8 pairs of gripper snaps and gripper snap tool

4" (10cm) of ¼" (3mm) wide elastic in a matching color to fabric C

Epoxy

½" (13mm) wide elastic, 4" (10cm) long

Core tools (page 106)

PATTERN (page 126)

FOLD-UP SPEAKER SET

It should be fairly easy to locate a fold-up speaker set that looks similar to the one below. Its portability (it is lightweight and battery-powered) and low cost make the set an ideal hacking material for Switch Crafting. During your search, you may find many being marketed as speakers designed for an iPod®, Zune®, or other media player. Don't be confused—they are essentially the same speaker set. Shop around for the best price.

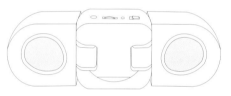

CUT OUT THE PATTERN

1. Mark and cut two Body pieces, two Straps, one Pocket Bottom, and one Pocket Top from fabric A. Mark and cut two Body pieces, two Straps, one Pocket Bottom, and four Dividers from fabric C. Cut out the Bucket pattern from fabric B. Cut out a Bucket and two Divider Centers from the Timtex.

2. If you are using a lightweight fabric for the exterior, interface the fabric A Body, Strap, and Pocket. If you've used a heavyweight fabric, such as barkcloth or denim, there is no need to line it.

3. With right sides together, sew the top ends of the two fabric A Straps to form one long Strap. Repeat with fabric C Straps to form one Lining Strap.

4. You'll need extra support in the Straps for the electronics. To do this, interface the Lining Strap, from the line marked on the strap down to the bottom, on both ends.

⚠ **CAUTION:** Before you start working on the speaker set, disconnect it from power and other devices. Make sure to remove the batteries as well. Also, visit our website to see step-by-step speaker hacking photos.

PREPARE THE SPEAKERS

5. Separate the two speakers from the amplifier. If your fold-up speaker set is similar to ours, do it this way: Remove the tray for the iPod and loosen the screws that hold the amplifier together (ours were hidden behind the battery compartment cover). Open up the amplifier, and you should see two hinges where the speakers connect to the amplifier. Gently remove the speakers from the hinges (A).

6. There should be two audio cables running between the amplifier and each speaker. If you see only one, carefully cut open a hole on the rubber casing around the wire; you are likely to see two wires underneath. Cut the audio cable for the left speaker at the center and mark the corresponding cable ends L1 and L2 on both sides. Also cut the two cables for the right speaker and mark them R1 and R2.

7. If your cut audio cables are really short, you will need to lengthen them. Do this by cutting eight 2"–4" (5–10cm) long wires and solder them individually to the four audio cable ends. The wires will need to be long enough to reach the back side of the amplifier and speakers (B).

8. Use hot glue to secure all solder joints. If your audio cables are very thin, add electrical tape to strengthen them—this helps keep the joint from breaking. Screw the amplifier back together. There will be four audio cables coming out from the holes created by the emptied hinges (C).

9. Attach the end of each audio cable to a "male" or stud gripper snap. See page 110 for instructions.

ADD THE ZIPPER

10. With right sides together, sew the Pocket to the Pocket Top, basting between the marks where the zipper will be located. Backstitch at the marks for stability and press the seams open.

11. Close the zipper. To make the zipper open to its proper length, loop a thread around the zipper teeth $14\frac{5}{8}$" (37cm) down from the top stop (D). Then, place the zipper face down and centered over the pressed seam allowance as marked (E).

> **TIP:** To keep a straight stitch line and avoid the pull tab on the zipper, start sewing at the bottom, then stop halfway up on the side, leave the needle in the fabric, and pull open the zipper three-fourths of the way down, then finish sewing. Repeat on the opposite side, but pull the zipper tab closed. There are many online sources that show how to sew a zipper. We like www.sewnews.com.

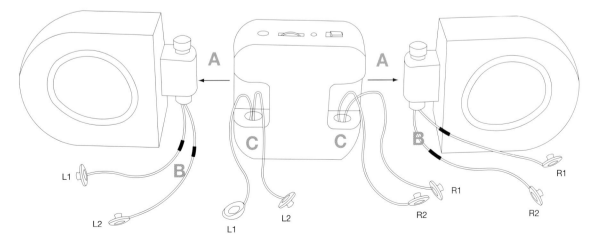

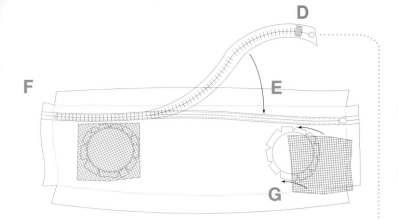

12. From the right side, use the zipper foot to stitch ⅛″ (3mm) around the zipper. Start by sewing across the bottom end, up one side, across the top end, and back down the other side **(F)**. Make sure to backstitch at each end. Take out the basting stitches you created in step 10.

COMPLETE THE POCKET

13. Cut out the speaker holes on the Exterior Pocket, notch the edges, fold the seam allowance back, and press it toward the wrong side. Baste stitch the 4″ x 4″ (10cm x 10cm) nylon mesh squares on the back of the circles, and topstitch them in place **(G)**.

14. With right sides facing, sew two Liner Divider pieces together at the 1″ (2.5cm) horizontal stitch line as marked on the pattern. Turn right side out and insert the Timtex Divider Center directly between the seams. On the right side, stitch vertically down the lining next to the Timtex, sealing it in be-

tween the two layers **(H)**. Fold each of the four flaps in half and topstitch. Press the seams open. It should look like the letter "I" from the side **(I)**. Repeat for the second Divider.

15. Cut out the speaker holes on the Pocket Lining. Use the same technique shown earlier in step 13. Pin and topstitch the Dividers onto the Lining as marked **(J)**.

16. Hand-stitch the top of the Pocket Lining to the underside of the zipper and to the seam allowance around the speaker holes. Machine-baste ¼″ (6mm) around the sides and bottom **(K)**.

MAKE THE BAG BODY

17. Cut two 11″ (28cm) and two 21″ (53.5cm) wires, preferably in different colors. Using sticky labels, mark the shorter wires R1 and R2, and mark the longer wires L1 and L2. Attach the end of each wire to the prong ring of a gripper snap (page 110). Do not attach the snap socket (the "female" gripper snap) to the prong ring yet.

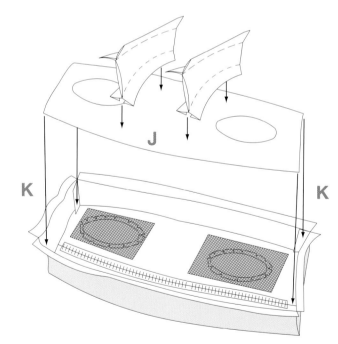

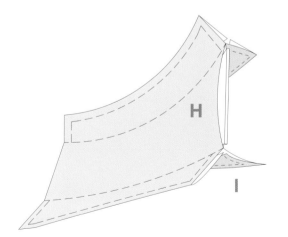

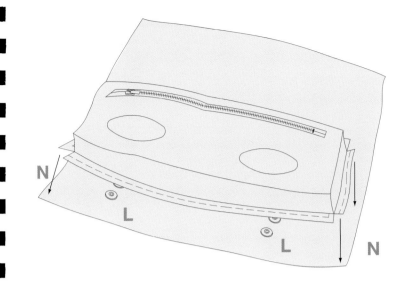

18. Pick one Exterior Body piece to be the Body Front. Take your soldered prong rings, and with the wires on the wrong-side and the snap sockets on the right-side, attach the prong right to the bag body at the marked areas **(L)**. Completely cover the rings and wires with hot glue on the wrong side, and sew the wires to the lining for secure placement **(M)**.

19. Fold under the seam allowance on the Pocket Top and press. Align and pin the bottom edge of the Pocket to the bottom edge of the Body Front. Topstitch the Pocket Top 1/8″ (3mm) and baste the sides and bottom 3/8″ (9.5mm) **(N)**. Hand-sew the Dividers to the Body Front as marked.

20. With right sides together, match the corners and topstitch the Strap to the edges of the Body Front and Body Back with a 1/2″ (13mm) seam **(O)**. With right sides together, stitch four 1/2″ (13mm) darts on the Bucket Exterior. Clip and press open. Match the corners and sew the Bucket onto the completed bag body **(P)**. Turn the bag right side out.

21. Score the Timtex Bucket piece lightly on the fold lines to make it easier to bend with a straight edge. Steam press the fold lines, sew the darts, and then trim the darts down to 1/8″ (3mm). Insert the Timtex Bucket into the bottom of the bag, fitting it snugly inside the Exterior Bucket. Using all-purpose thread, tack the darts of the Timtex Bucket to the darts of the Bucket for extra support.

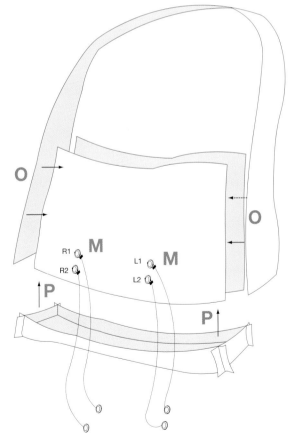

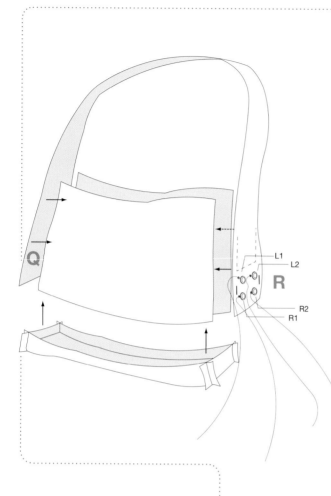

PUT IT ALL TOGETHER

24. Fold and press the seam allowances of the Lining Body and Bag Body inward 1/2" (13mm). Insert the Lining into the Bag with wrong sides together. Use electrical tape to hold the wires in place at the bottom of the bag **(S)**.

25. Place the amplifier against the socket snaps where it will eventually be snapped into the bag **(T)**. Using a permanent marker, mark the location where the socket snaps fit against the amplifier. Use this mark to position where to epoxy your stud snaps. Now, use epoxy to affix the stud snaps to the marks, and let the epoxy cure according to its directions. After the epoxy dries, tape down the wires **(U)**. Repeat this step with your two speakers **(V)**.

26. Topstitch the Lining to the Bag and the Strap, insert the batteries, and snap in your amplifier and speakers. Use the 1/2" (13mm) wide elastic to hold the amplifier in place.

CREATE THE LINING BODY

22. Using fabric C, make a Player Pocket based on the size of your music player with the patch pocket technique (page 109). Sew the Pocket to the Lining Strap as indicated on the pattern. Machine-stitch the 1/4" (3mm) wide elastic into place as marked. With right sides facing, sew the Lining Strap, Lining Body, and Lining Bucket together, like you did for the Exterior Bag Body **(Q)**.

23. With the wires on the wrong side, attach the L1, L2, R1, and R2 rings to the snap sockets through the Body. After testing for continuity with your multimeter (page 108), completely cover the rings and wires with hot glue on the wrong side. Sew the wires to the lining for secure placement **(R)**.

↻ remix

- Try a larger speaker set for more powerful sound. You will probably have to adjust the pattern to accommodate larger speakers.
- Add piping to the edges of the bag, as shown in the photos.
- Use waterproof materials and make a boom box beach bag. You may have to move the speaker pocket up or into the bag to avoid water or sand.

USE & CARE

>> Place your media player in the inside pocket, and connect it to the amplifier (an extension cable may be needed for the connection if yours is too short). Turn on the media player and amplifier and you are ready to play.

>> Remove the amplifier and speakers before washing by hand.

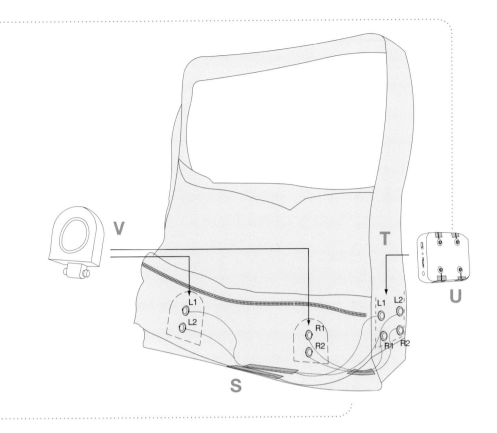

"ghettoblaster"

The ghettoblaster, a.k.a. boombox, was introduced in the mid 1970s. It brought forth the idea of a personal portable stereo. What's more, its portability and early design emphasis on producing music at a loud volume took the personal music experience to the streets. The ghettoblaster is thus an extension of the time-honored tradition of communal entertainment that helps in building and maintaining shared cultural memory. It is also defiant and forever linked to the early days of hip-hop music and break dancing, as evidenced in Spike Lee's *Do the Right Thing*. In the hey days of boombox, it was a status symbol of urban culture, and the manufacturers were tripping over themselves to offer the baddest and the flashiest of systems. That heady time is no more. However, with the boost from new technologies such as satellite radio and iPod docks, new generations of boomboxes live on.

Chapter Three: Work It

These projects do the job every time, with style.

PRIVACY
PASSPORT COVER

catch me if you can

There is a radio chip in every new U.S. passport that transmits your passport and personal information to the wireless readers at passport checkpoints. This passport cover cloaks the tracking signal, hiding it from any would-be thieves. Never let anyone discover your mysterious globe-trotting ways!

[CRAFT] ■ ▫ ▫   [TECH] ■ ▫ ▫   [COST] ■ ▫ ▫

[MATERIALS & TOOLS]

FABRIC A, EXTERIOR: 9" x 7" (23cm x 18cm) of a medium-weight fabric, such as cotton, polyester, or linen

FABRIC B, INTERIOR: 13" x 9" (33cm x 23cm) of a medium-weight fabric, such as cotton, polyester, or linen

Plastic self-adhesive liner, such as Kittrich Magic Cover®

8" x 8" (20.5cm x 20.5cm) aluminum foil

All-purpose thread to match fabric B

Grosgrain ribbon, twill tape, or bias tape to match fabric B

Core tools (page 106)

PATTERN (page 129)

1. Trace and cut out the Passport Body piece from fabric A, fabric B, aluminum foil, and plastic liner. Cut out two Passport Flaps from fabric B.

2. Cut away the 1/2" (13mm) seam allowance from the foil and place it on the sticky side of the plastic liner. Cut away the edges of the liner, leaving a 1/8" (3mm) edge around the foil **(A)**.

3. Sandwich the foil-liner layer between the wrong sides of the Body pieces. Sew the Body pieces together with a 1/8" (3mm) seam allowance, securing the foil and liner inside the Body **(B)**.

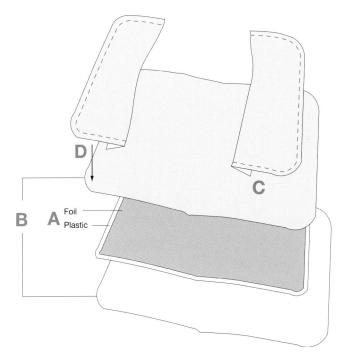

USE & CARE

>> Put your passport in the cover before hitting the road.

>> Take your passport out of the cover before handing it to an immigration officer.

↻ remix

• If you have a credit card or ID card with an RFID chip in it, you may want to make a carrier for it too.

4. Fold and press both Passport Flaps back ½" (13mm), folding them toward the wrong side at the marked fold line **(C)**.

5. With the wrong side of the Flaps facing the right side of the Passport Body, sew both flaps with ⅛" (3mm) seam allowance around the outside edge of the Passport Body **(D)**.

6. Press the grosgrain ribbon in half lengthwise and pick a point near a Flap on the bottom edge. Starting at this point, machine stitch the ribbon around the edges of the cover. Make sure the head and tail of the ribbon are folded back. Hand-stitch the ends.

RFID and your privacy

The radio-frequency identification (RFID) tag is a small device that stores information; it can be just a simple ID number or as extensive as a patient's medical history. It has been used for cattle tracking, and has found its way into supply chain management systems, credit cards, student IDs, and more. Some fashion brands also use RFID systems to keep track of your preferences and purchase history. Next time you are in Manhattan, check out the Prada store in SoHo: It takes RFID technology to the next level by using the tags to recommend accessories that match your outfit, show the runway video of your chosen product, and more.

In 2006, the U.S. government began embedding an RFID tag in the US passport. Predictably, a controversy regarding individual privacy broke out, and this argument still rages on today. This is a complex issue, and we can see the merits in the arguments from both sides. If you care about your privacy or simply want to learn more about potential applications of RFID from a design standpoint, we encourage you to research the topic and decide for yourself.

FASHION WITH
SECRET IPOD AND
EARBUD HOLDER

iHoodie

The iHoodie is a smart, stylish, sleeveless hoodie that hides away your mp3 player and headphones with chic convenience. Keep yourself warm and cozy in a cool breeze, and walk down the street to your own beats.

iHoodie

[CRAFT] ■ ■ ▢   [TECH] ■ ▢ ▢   [COST] ■ ▢ ▢

[MATERIALS & TOOLS]

iPod nano or your favorite MP3 player

FABRIC A, EXTERIOR: 6½ yd (2.3m) of 60" wide jersey, interlock, or velour knit

FABRIC B, POCKET FACING AND BAND: 1 yd (0.9m) cotton or medium-weight jersey knit

All-purpose thread to match fabric A and B

¼" (6mm) wide elastic, 6" (15cm) long

Binding (bias tape), 8½' (2.6m) long in complementary color to fabric A

3 yd (2.7m) of knit ribbing in matching or complementary color to fabric B.

Core tools (page 106)

PATTERN (page 130)

TIP: The sleeveless hoodie pattern on page 130 is a women's size small to medium, but since jersey fabric stretches, it will fit a wider range of sizes. If you're not up for sewing the hoodie from scratch, any store-bought one will work. Just sew the elastic strips in step 3 to the inside hood seam (C), and sew a Player Pocket in step 6 (F) to the inside of the hoodie pockets.

1. Mark and cut out two Pocket Facings, two Hoods, one Back, and one Front from fabric A. Mark and cut out one Player Pocket, two Pocket Linings, and one Lower Band from fabric B. Cut three 2" (5cm) elastic strips. Cut two 25" (63.5cm) bindings and one 52" (1.3m) binding.

2. Decide if you want your MP3 Player Pocket on the left or right side.

3. Fold the elastic strips in half and pin them to the wrong side of the Front, as marked on the pattern (two on the neck seam, and one below either the left or right armhole depending on which side you have your MP3 player). With right sides together, sew Front and Back shoulders together with a ½" (13mm) seam **(A)**. Do the same for the two Hood pieces **(B)**.

4. Sew the completed Hood to the neck seam, right sides together. This locks in the two elastic strips on the neck seam, facing inside **(C)**. Sew the 52" (1.3m) binding around the hood and neckline, starting and ending at the center front. Sew each 25" (1.3m) binding around the armholes, starting at the inside seam Front and ending at the inside seam Back. Cut off excess bindings **(D)**.

5. Pin and machine-sew the Pocket Facings, right sides together, to both sides of the Hoodie Front between the notches. Clip the seam allowance to the notches **(E)**. Press the Facings to the wrong side of the Hoodie Front, keeping the rest of the seam allowance flipped out.

6. Create the buttonhole on the Pocket Lining on either your left or right pocket, depending on your preference. Press the edges of the Player Pocket under ½" (13mm). Pin and top-stitch the Player Pocket to the Lining as marked **(F)**.

↺ remix

- If your media player is not a first- or second-generation iPod nano, adjust the size of the inside pocket to fit your player.
- For added convenience and control, you may cut holes for the iPod display and the control wheel on the Nano pocket.
- If you don't want to make a hoodie from scratch, try adding the pocket and the elastic strips to your favorite hoodie.

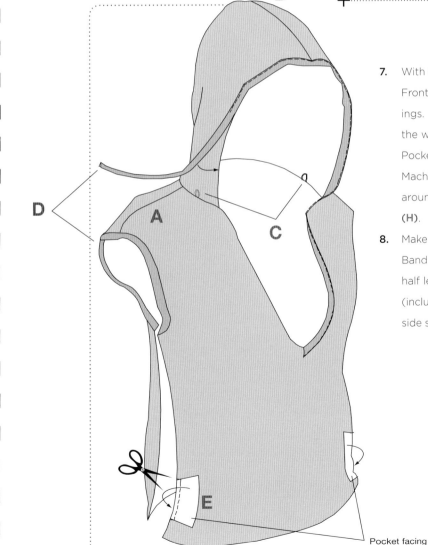

Pocket facing

7. With right sides together, pin and stitch the sides of Hoodie Front and Back pieces together, avoiding the pocket openings. **(G)** With the right side of the Pocket Lining facing the wrong side of the Front, align the bottom edges of the Pocket Linings to the bottom edge of the Hoodie Front. Machine-stitch the Pocket Linings to the Hoodie Front around the arced seam line, leaving the bottom edges open **(H)**.

8. Make a continuous band by sewing the ends of the Lower Band together with a ½" (13mm) seam. Press the Band in half lengthwise and sew it to the bottom edge of the Body (including Pocket Linings) with right sides together and the side seams aligned.

USE & CARE

>> Remove iPod and earbuds before washing, and wash as directed by fabric specifications.

9. Reinforce the Pockets at the top and the bottom of the opening with a ¾" (2cm) stitch at each notch.

10. Running your headphone wires from the inside of the Hoodie, pull the headphone jack through the buttonhole to rest in the Player Pocket. Then thread the earbuds through the armhole strap and pull one through each Hood strap.

11. Insert your MP3 Player into the Player Pocket and plug in the headphone jack.

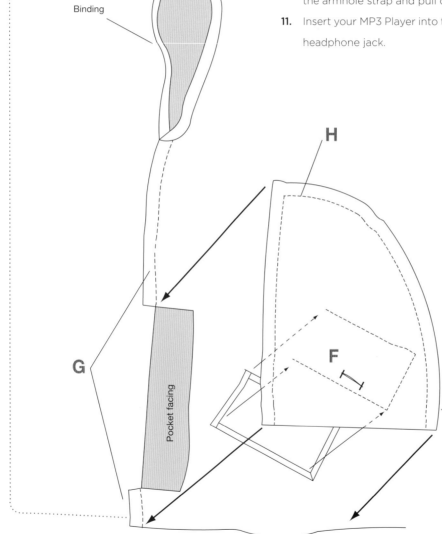

Binding

H

G

Pocket facing

F

NEWSBOY CAP FOR IPOD SHUFFLE

petal shuffle

"Extra! Extra! Hear all about it!" Look good while hiding away your iPod shuffle in a stylish newsboy cap. Controls are built into the flower petals so you can change the volume or switch songs with a flip of your finger.

petal shuffle

[CRAFT] ◼ ▢ ▢   **[TECH]** ◼ ▢ ▢   **[COST]** ◼ ▢ ▢

[MATERIALS & TOOLS]

FABRIC A, EXTERIOR: 1/2 yd (45.5cm) of medium-weight fabric such as cotton or a silk blend

FABRIC B, LINING: 1/2 yd (45.5cm) of medium-weight woven fabric of your choice

FABRIC C, FLOWER: 5" x 7" (12.5cm x 18cm) wool felt or felted cashmere

Timtex™ interfacing, 16" x 3" (40.5 cm 7.5cm)

All-purpose thread to match fabrics A and B

Small glass, plastic, or crystal jewelry beads

Core tools (page 106)

PATTERN (page 129)

PREPARE THE PATTERN

1. Mark and cut four Hat Panels from fabric A and four from fabric B. Also mark and cut two Hat Brims from fabric A and one from the Timtex, one Hat Pocket from fabric A, and one Small and Large Flower from fabric C.

MAKE THE CROWN AND THE BRIM

2. With right sides together, sew all four Panels at adjacent edges with a 1/2" (13mm) seam. Repeat with the lining, leaving two 1/2" (13mm) openings over the ears as marked on the pattern **(A)**. Press the seams open and snip off extra fabric from the tip to prevent bunching **(B)**.

3. Create a buttonhole on the hat exterior fabric as marked **(C)**.

4. With right sides together, sew the curved edge of the Brim. Turn right side out and insert the Timtex piece. Press. Sew the Brim to the outside of the hat, sealing the Timtex inside **(D)**.

5. Create a patch pocket (page 109) from the Hat Pocket piece, and topstitch it to the outside of the hat as marked on the pattern **(E)**.

6. With right sides together, sew the lining to the hat, leaving a 1" (2.5cm) opening at the back. Turn right side out, press, and topstitch around the seam.

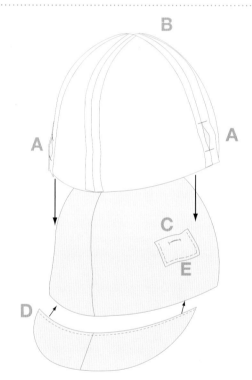

↺ remix

*   If your audio player is not a second-generation iPod shuffle, you may be able to modify the pattern to fit your player, as long as it is not too large or heavy.

*   Play with the designs of the cap and the flower. Try adding other ornaments.

CREATE THE FLOWER

7. Cut out the center circle and slice the lines radiating from the center on the Large Flower pattern. Fold each petal in half, and sew the dart as marked (F).

8. Bead the Small Flower by pulling a thread up through the fabric, stringing on a bead, and then pulling the thread back down through the fabric. Repeat until you finish the pattern (G). Hand-sew the Small Flower to the center of the Large Flower.

9. With the headphone jack on top, place your iPod shuffle into the pocket. Center the flower directly over the play button and align the bead rows over each of the controls: volume up, volume down, next, and previous (H). Test the controls by pushing on the beads. If you've assembled the hat correctly, you should hear a click from the iPod Shuffle. Remove the Shuffle and stitch the flower into place.

PUT THEM TOGETHER

10. Insert the earbuds between the lining and exterior through the opening in the back. Thread the jack through the buttonhole and each earbud through the side seam openings of the lining. Stuff the rest of the headphone wires in the back of the hat and slip stitch shut. Or add a fabric snap in the back if you want the earbuds to be removable.

11. Put your iPod Shuffle in the pocket and plug in the headphone jack.

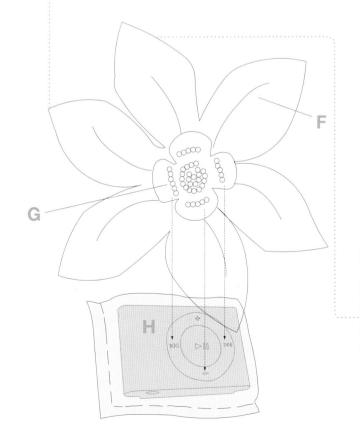

USE & CARE

>> Press the beads on the flower to control your iPod shuffle.
>> Remove the earbuds and player before cleaning as suggested by fabric specifications. Be careful of the flower.

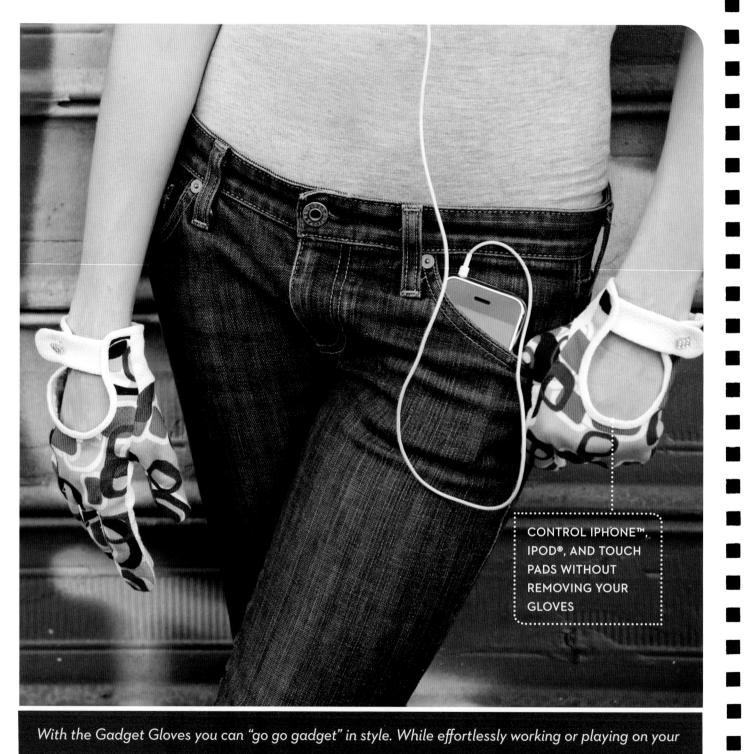

CONTROL IPHONE™, IPOD®, AND TOUCH PADS WITHOUT REMOVING YOUR GLOVES

With the Gadget Gloves you can "go go gadget" in style. While effortlessly working or playing on your electronic gizmo, you never have to surrender your hands to the cold again. Even Carrie Bradshaw would approve of these stylish gloves.

gadget gloves

[CRAFT] ■ ■ ■   [TECH] ■ ■ ■   [COST] ■ ■ ■

[MATERIALS & TOOLS]

FABRIC A, OUTER GLOVE AND THUMB: 1/4 yd (23cm) patterned no-stretch cotton

FABRIC B, PALM AND GUSSETS: 1 yd (91cm) solid no-stretch cotton

THREAD A: all-purpose silk or polyester thread to match Fabric B

THREAD B: conductive thread (page 104)

1 sew-on snap, size: 1/0

Decorative button of your choice

Core tools (page 106)

PATTERN (page 136)

CUT THE PATTERN

1. Cut out two Outer Glove and two Thumb pieces from fabric A. Cut two Palms, two Bias Trims, four Straps, two Gusset As, and four Gusset Bs from fabric B.

> **⊹ IMPORTANT: Ensuring the Gloves Fit**
> The pattern is designed for a small- to medium-sized female hand. If you are not sure about the size, make one out of sample fabric, such as muslin, first. To improve the fit, adjust the pattern pieces to your size and measurements, making most adjustments to the length and width of the gussets. A good reference site on how to make and fit gloves is www.glove.org.

CREATE THE BODY AND THE THUMB

2. With the right sides of one Outer Glove and one Palm together, sew 1/8" (3mm) along the inner side (forefinger/thumb) seam: Start at the midpoint of the forefinger fingertip, sew down to the top of the thumbhole, stop, and then sew from the bottom of the thumbhole down to the wrist. Press open **(A)**.

3. Fold one Thumb piece in half, right sides together, and sew along the side seam. Turn right side out.

A

4. With the Thumb piece right side out and the glove wrong side up, insert the Thumb into the thumbhole. Take extra care to match up the notches on the Thumb exactly to the thumb-hole notches on the Palm **(B)**. Line up the raw edges, and sew a 1/8" (3mm) seam. This is similar to sewing a set-in sleeve on a garment.

5. Sew the right side of one Bias Trim to the right side of the glove along the wrist of the Palm, around the bottom edge of the Outer Glove, and around the button tab. Fold and press it back onto itself, wrapping around the raw edge of the glove, and topstitch into place **(C)**. Now turn the Thumb wrong side out.

![icon] **IMPORTANT: Precision**

Inserting gussets requires precision. Be sure to always match up the markings for each gusset before sewing, follow the order of attachment in the following steps, and test the fit after each gusset is sewn.

SEW THE GUSSETS

6. With right sides together, sew one Gusset B between the index finger and middle finger of the Outer Glove. Sew from the midpoint of the index fingertip to the midpoint of the middle fingertip **(D)**. Repeat on the Palm side. Repeat this technique by sewing a Gusset B between the middle and ring fingers **(E)**.

    ![icon] **TIP:** Pull the middle finger back while sewing down the index finger to keep it out of the way. Stop, and then pin and sew the gusset the rest of the way up the middle finger. This tip can be applied to other fingers too.

7. Sew the outside seam on the side with the pinky finger. Start from the wrist up to the midpoint of the pinky fingertip **(F)**. Sew in Gusset A between the ring and pinky finger following the same gusset-sewing technique **(G)**.

8. Turn the glove right side out. Some trimming of the seam may be needed for it to fit smoothly in the fingertips.

ADD THE STRAP

9. Sew two Strap pieces right sides together, but leave an opening at the straight end. Turn right side out. Stitch the strap to the wrong side of the glove at the outer edge of the Bias Seam **(H)**.

10. Put on the glove, and mark where you want the snap on the strap. Hand-sew a pair of snaps to the front side of the Outer Glove and the back side of the Strap at your marks **(I)**. Finish by adding a decorative button on the front side of the strap **(J)**.

PUT IT ALL TOGETHER

11. Put on the glove again and simulate operating your touch-sensitive device. With a fabric pen, mark the spot on the tip of the index finger and thumb that has the most control over your device.

12. Hand-sew conductive thread in a ¼" x ¼" (6mm x 6mm) square at the mark on the index finger as follows: Sew a set of horizontal stitches into a square and then cross over the sewn square with a set of vertical stitches **(K)**. Make sure there is an equal amount of thread on both the right and wrong sides of the fabric. Now sew another square of conductive thread at the mark on the thumb by repeating the stitching process.

13. Repeat steps 2 through 12 for the other glove.

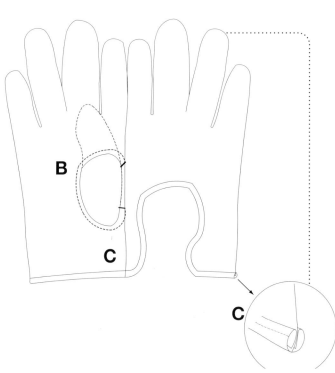

USE & CARE

>> Follow the wash and care instructions for your fabric.

>> The conductive thread may get a little tarnished over time. Don't over-wash.

↺ remix

- If you don't want to make your own, stitch conductive squares to your favorite pair of gloves.
- Instead of the small conductive square, try making a large conduct area with conductive fabric.

how gadget gloves work

When people tell you that you are electric, they are not only talking about your style. The human body, including the fingers, is actually conductive and stores electrons. This electron-storing ability is called capacitance. Most touchpads and touchscreens used in the latest gadgets work by creating a capacitance field on their surface. The field gets distorted whenever your finger touches it. The position and motion of the finger is then computed by the device so that it's able to direct the cursor or make selections. This is not possible when you have thick gloves on. The conductive thread that we added to the Gadget Gloves eliminates the problem.

LAPTOP BAG
THAT PROTECTS
AND DETECTS
WI-FI HOTSPOTS

galaxy carrier 802.11

Be the queen of the galaxy with this space-age satellite Wi-Fi detecting bag. With a simple push of a button, your Galaxy Carrier will light up, alerting you to a Wi-Fi hotspot without you having to open your laptop. Inspired by the sci-fi cult figure Barbarella, this stylish laptop bag also protects your computer on the go.

[CRAFT] ■ ■   [TECH] ■   [COST] ■ ■

[MATERIALS & TOOLS]

FABRIC A, BODY: 1½ yd (1.4m) middleweight vinyl with cotton backing. If you don't like vinyl, pick a sturdy material like barkcloth.

FABRIC B, HANDLE: ¼ yd (23cm) medium-weight fabric. We used a coated linen for contrast.

FABRIC C, LINING: 2 yd (1.8m) lightweight cotton or similar fabric. We used Futurella fabric from Alexander Henry.

2 yd (1.8m) of ½" (13mm) cotton batting

¼ yd (23cm) Timtex™ interfacing. If you want more handle support, you will need an extra ¼ yd (23cm).

Fusible appliqué paper

Wi-Fi detector (see sidebar below)

Heavy-duty thread to match fabric A

All-purpose thread to match fabric B

Leather machine needle

Core tools (page 106)

PATTERN SCHEMATIC (page 133)

WI-FI HOTSPOT DETECTOR

....

At the touch of a button, a Wi-Fi detector shows you the presence and signal strength of a wireless hotspot, thus saving you the hassle of taking out a notebook computer for the same purpose. Since most detectors provide pretty much the same functionality, we like the older, discontinued models that are sold at a lower price. Try finding them in brick-and-mortar discounters or from an online source such as eBay or Amazon. Look for a detector that is thin, possesses a large detection button, and has decent space between the button and the indicator lights for more design freedom.

CUT THE PATTERN

1. Our pattern is designed for a laptop that is 1" x 14" x 9½" (2.5cm x 35.5cm x 24.4cm). Measure your laptop's length, width, and height to ensure a good fit and make any adjustments to the pattern pieces before cutting.

2. Cut and mark two Body pieces from fabric A, two Handles from both fabric B and the Timtex (optional: cut two extra Timtex Handles), and cut two Lining pieces from fabric C and from the batting.

 TIP: Body pattern width = laptop width + depth + ½" (13mm) seam allowance. Body pattern height = height + depth + ½" (13mm) seam allowance. Also modify Handle and Lining widths on the pattern pieces accordingly.

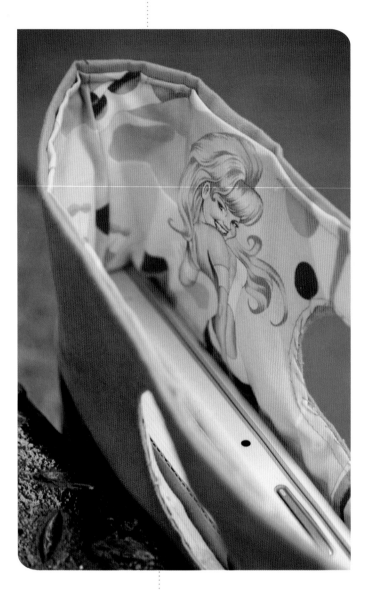

PREPARE THE DETECTOR PATCH

3. Cut out an interesting shape or image to use as the appliqué on the front of the bag. Using your Wi-Fi detector as a reference, trace and cut out a button shape (we used a star) that covers the size of the button on the Wi-Fi detector.

 TIP: You can also use a clothing button as the button for the Wi-Fi detector.

4. Arrange the cut pieces onto the fusible appliqué, paper side up, with the Wi-Fi detector underneath. Align and pin the button shape over the detector button, and also align your appliqué design over the Wi-Fi indicator lights so that they will light up in a creative way—ours shine through the windows on a rocket. Follow the instructions for your fusible appliqué paper to bond the shapes together. Decide the shape of your Patch and cut it out **(A)**.

5. Using the Lining fabric, make a patch pocket for your Wi-Fi detector with $1/2''$ (13mm) seam allowance (page 109) **(B)**.

6. Align, mark, and pin these elements in place: the Patch, one fabric B Handle piece, one Timtex Handle piece (optional: use two for extra support), Wi-Fi detector, and the Pocket. It is important to line up the lights and the button with your appliqué design. Make sure the Pocket does not go past a $5/8''$ (15.9mm) clearance under the $1/2''$ (13mm) seam line of the Handle's top and side edges **(C)**.

7. Mark and cut a hole for the detector's light row from the Timtex and fabric B pieces. Mark and cut a hole for the button from the Timtex piece **(D)**.

8. Once everything is aligned and ready, sew the Pocket with all-purpose thread to the wrong side of the Timtex, then iron the Patch to the right side of the Handle, following the directions for your appliqué paper.

MAKE THE HANDLES AND BAG

9. Cut the handle holes on both fabric Handle pieces, and snip to the seam line. Do not press flat to the wrong side yet **(E)**. Also cut the handle hole on each Timtex piece and cut away ¼" (6mm) from four sides **(F)**.

10. Baste ¼" (6mm) around the edges of the Timtex (one layer or two) to the fabric Handle. Trim the edges of Timtex as close to the seams as possible, so that later it won't interfere with the side seams. Press the snipped seam allowance of the fabric B Handle Hole to the wrong side of the Timtex. Repeat this step to make the other Handle.

> ✻ **TIP:** When aligning this many elements together, it will take a few attempts—be patient. You may ask a friend to help, use straight pins to hold things together while working, or have a fabric-marking pen right next to you to mark the locations of important elements.

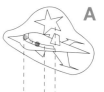

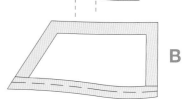

802.11, airport, and wi-fi: what's in a name?

You may not have heard of 802.11 but you most likely know it as Wi-Fi or Air-Port. The lowdown is that 802.11 is the name of a set of technical standards for wireless local area networks (WLANs). There are different versions, such as 802.11b, 802.11g, 802.11n. Each signifies a distinct standard which dictates the speed at which they carry data and the frequency they run on. So what's up with the schizophrenic nomenclature? We venture to guess that one of the main reasons is marketability. A rose by any other name may smell as sweet, but you sure can sell it for a different price.

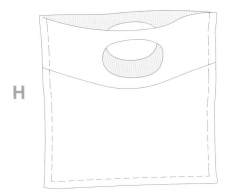

G

H

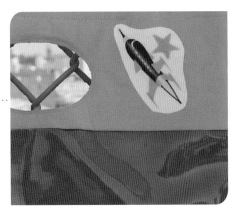

11. With right sides together, align and sew one Handle to each Body using heavy-duty thread (G). Flip handles up, and sew the newly created Bodies with right sides together, using heavy-duty thread (H). Turn right side out.

12. Using all-purpose thread, baste the batting to the wrong side of the Lining pieces at the seam lines. Trim the seam if needed. Sew the Linings together with right sides facing, and clip the corners (I). Cut out the handle holes from the Lining, and then clip, fold, and press the seam allowances to the wrong side.

13. Fold the top edges of the Body ½" (13mm) to the wrong side and topstitch with all-purpose thread, ⅜" (10mm) around the edge (J).

PUT THEM TOGETHER

14. Turn the Lining's top edges ½" (13mm) to the wrong side (K). With wrong sides facing, insert the Lining into the Body, and topstitch around the top of the Bag in the same ⅜" (10mm) stitch that you just sewed. Leave an opening at the Detector Pocket.

15. Pin and topstitch around the Handle Holes. Insert your Wi-Fi detector.

↺ remix

- To give the button a better feel, make the shape over the button with multiple layers.
- Apply a sheet of iron-on vinyl over the patch for protection and an enhanced look.

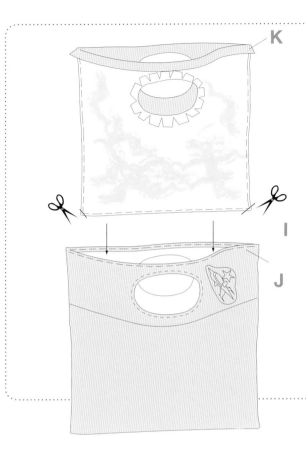

K

I

J

USE & CARE

>> Press the shape over the button to activate the Wi-Fi detector. Refer to its manual for the meaning of the indicator lights.

>> Use the bag as a laptop sleeve by folding the handles to one side after you put your computer in the bag. It can also serve as a pad when you use the laptop on your thighs, assuming the laptop doesn't become too hot for your fabric.

>> Remove the detector before cleaning. Follow the wash and care instructions for your fabric.

>> See the Wi-Fi detector's manual for how to change batteries.

women in sci-fi

Even though Mary Shelley wrote one of the world's first science fiction novels, Frankenstein, the sci-fi genre—let's be honest—has traditionally been "a guy thing." There are only so many damsels in distress that one can take. Luckily, female sci-fi writers have been increasing their influence since the late 1960s. Many writers have taken advantage of the fictional nature of the genre to explore gender roles and social conventions. Coupled with the advancement of gender equality in our society, stronger female sci-fi characters such as Ellen Ripley (*Alien*) and Buffy the Vampire Slayer have been embraced by pop culture. From sex symbols to femme fatales, women in sci-fi have come a long way.

To learn more, check out the books *Decoding Gender in Science Fiction*, by Brian Attebery, and *Fantasy Girls: Gender in the New Universe of Science Fiction and Fantasy Television*, by Elyce Rae Helford. Next time a sci-fi heroine comes blazing to a theater screen near you, bring your friends and show off all your sci-fi knowledge—popcorn optional.

SCENTED AUTOMATIC WARDROBE OR DRAWER LAMP

Keep your prized delicates smelling good with the Aromatherapy Sachet. It is also an automatic lamp with a hidden image that amazes. Have one in every drawer, wardrobe, and closet and see the once dark space illuminated when opened. You can now find things with ease with an added enchanting bouquet of fragrance.

aromatherapy sachet

[CRAFT] ▪ ☐ ☐   [TECH] ▪ ▪ ☐   [COST] ▪ ☐ ☐

[MATERIALS & TOOLS]

FABRIC A, SIDES AND BACK: 8″ x 8″ (20.5cm x 20.5cm) of medium-weight fabric, such as cotton, wool felt, or linen

FABRIC B, TOP PANEL: 4″ x 4″ (10cm x 10cm) lightweight rayon that is opaque but allows light to shine through

FABRIC C, INTERIOR: 4″ x 4″ (10cm x 10cm) piece of tulle

4½″ x 4½″ (11.5cm x 11.5cm) fabric squares in variety of colors. OUR SUGGESTIONS: fluorescent pink for the sun and sun rays, fluorescent orange for the sun backdrop, light lavender for the land, and wine for the birds.

All-purpose thread to match fabric B

¾″ (2cm) wide sew-on Velcro

4″ x 3½″ (10cm x 9cm) piece of cardboard

Three-LED Button with Reflective Cone: viewing angle, 5mm, wide viewing angle, 3–4 volt

Cotton balls

Scented essential oil, scent of your choice

Magnetic switch, normally-closed type (page 105)

Core tools (page 106)

PATTERN (page 137)

CUT THE PATTERN

1. Mark and cut out one Sachet Body and one Side Panel from fabric A. Cut out two Top Panels from fabric B and one Top Panel from fabric C. Cut out all the template pieces (sun, rays, backdrop, land, birds) from the fabric squares.

2. Cut a 4″ (10cm) piece of ¾″ (2cm) wide Velcro, then cut it in half length-wise, making it ⅜″ (9.5mm) wide.

CREATE THE BODY

3. Avoiding the seam allowance, sew one strip of Velcro to the right side of the Side Panel and the other strip to the right side of the Sachet Body as indicated on the pattern. Attach the Side Panel to the Body by pressing the two pieces of Velcro together **(A)**.

4. On the Sachet Body, sew the adjacent edges together to make four square corners **(B)**.

MAKE THE TOP PANEL

5. Organize the template pieces on the wrong side of one of the rayon Top Panels as shown in the diagram. Sew the template pieces in the following order: the sun backdrop, the land, the sun, and the rays. Glue on the birds **(C)**.

6. Sandwich and sew the designed Top Panel between the tulle and the other Top Panel with a ¼″ (6mm) seam **(D)**.

7. On the wrong side of this new Top Panel, machine stitch around the sun and across the horizon according to the Final Stitch Template (page 137).

8. With right sides together, sew the Top Panel onto the Sachet Body. Make sure the bottom of the template image is on the Velcro side of the Body **(E)**.

✳ **IMPORTANT: Making the design light friendly**
The key to an attractive design that glows is to make things translucent but to use a few opaque accent pieces to create shadows. To enhance the "wow" factor, keep the right side of the Top Panel as minimal as possible, with only a few decorative stitch lines, so that it doesn't give away what happens when the light is on.

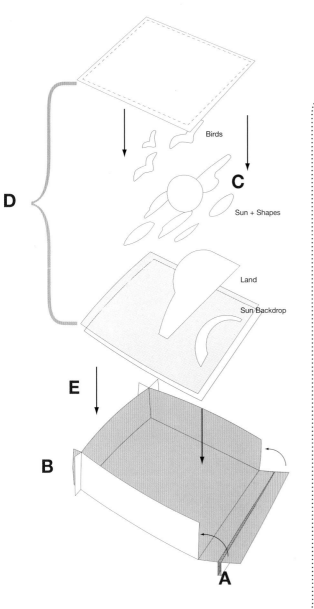

Birds

C

Sun + Shapes

D

Land

Sun Backdrop

E

B

A

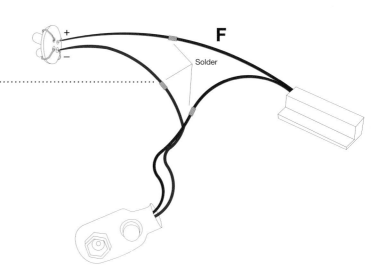

F

Solder

+

−

CREATE THE SCENTED LIGHT BOARD

9. Make an LED Button with 3 LEDs and the reflective cone according to the instructions on pages 117–118.

10. Cut the wires of the magnetic switch to 4" (10cm). Solder the [+] leg of the LED Button to one wire of the switch, and solder the [+] wire of the battery snap to the other wire of the switch. Solder the [−] leg of the LED Button to the [−] wire of the battery snap **(F)**. Cover the base of the button and wrap all other soldering joints with electrical tape.

11. Hot glue the LED Button to the center of the cardboard piece **(G)**. If you want this to be a drawer sachet, glue the switch horizontally to the top center of the cardboard as illustrated **(H)**. If you're using the sachet in the wardrobe or cabinet, place the switch vertically on the upper left or upper right corner depending on what side of the door it will be next to.

12. Let the 9-volt battery snap hang near the side with the Velcro. Secure all loose wires to the cardboard with electronic tape.

13. Squeeze a single (and rather frugal) drop of scented essential oil onto 8 individual cotton balls. Leave them sitting for a few hours to absorb.

IMPORTANT: Keep It Clean

To ensure that none of the essential oil comes into contact with your fabric, you can glue a clean cotton ball to each oiled cotton ball. Affix it onto the exact spot where the oil was dropped to cover the stain. Try not to put glue directly on the oil but around the spot. Don't overdo it—you want to keep the cotton balls fluffy so that the scent can diffuse better.

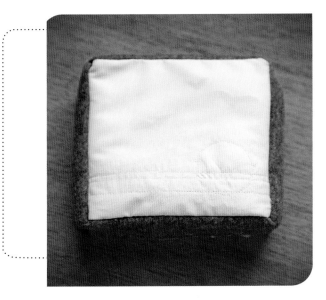

USE & CARE

>> To wash, take out the cardboard with electronics, remove the cotton balls, and hand-wash based on the washing instructions for your materials.

I

H

G

↻ remix

- If you'd like to hang the sachet (if your drawer is too deep, for instance), add Velcro or a string to the back of your sachet and hang it in place.
- Try different scents for different aromatherapy benefits.
- Design your own lighting panel.

FINISH THE SACHET

14. Insert the Light Board into the Body, with the light facing the Sachet Top. Note that the 9-volt battery snap should be just right inside the Velcro opening **(I)**. Stuff the cotton balls around the light cone. Add more cotton balls if needed.

15. Hook up the battery, and place the sachet in your wardrobe, drawer, or cabinet. Attach the unwired half of the magnetic switch to your wardrobe, cabinet door, or the surface above your drawer. Make sure the position of the switch is close enough to the hidden switch inside the Sachet to turn off the light when the door is shut or the drawer is closed.

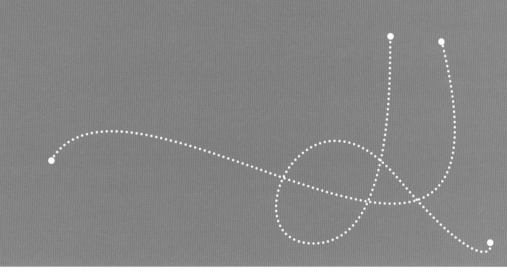

Chapter Four: Play Hard

Life isn't all work. Have some fun with projects that bring play into your day.

TOY WITH
SOUND-BITE

The "Bad Boy" Dog Toy, made from your old T-shirt and jeans, will make your puppy go wild. Watch ears perk up from uninhibited enjoyment as the toy plays a sound every time it's chewed. Don't tame your Bad Boy—give him a toy.

"bad boy" dog toy

[CRAFT] ▢ ▢ [TECH] ▢ ▢ ▢ [COST] ▢ ▢ ▢

[MATERIALS & TOOLS]

FRONT: old cotton T-shirt with a cool silk-screened image; see step 1 of instructions

FABRIC A, BACK: old pair of jeans, size determined by T-shirt image

FABRIC B, BACKING: medium-weight fabric such as cotton, canvas, or denim, size determined by T-shirt image

THREAD A: all-purpose thread in matching color to fabric A or T-shirt

THREAD B: topstitching thread in contrasting color to fabric A

Sound kit (at right), sound of your choice

Cotton stuffing

Core tools (page 106)

PUSH-ACTIVATED SOUND KIT

One fun way to liven up your creations is to add some interesting, if not hilarious, interactive sound effects. You may have noticed those make-your-own-stuffed-animal shops popping up in your area and online. Many of them sell sound kits/chips that purr, roar, or sing with just a press or squeeze of the hand.

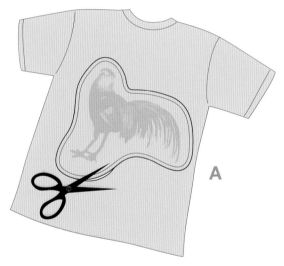

A

B

1. When picking out a T-shirt, make sure your design makes a toy that is size appropriate for your dog—do not make it too small or with pieces he can ingest or swallow. With a fabric pen, draw a smooth, flowing line on your T-shirt completely around your image. Make sure the line is at least ½" (13mm) away from the image edge.

2. Measure and mark a line ½" (13mm) out from the line you just drew for the seam allowance, and cut the shape out. This will be the Toy Front (A).

⚠ CAUTION: Dog Toy Safety

The ASPCA recommends the following when giving pets toys:

- You should always monitor your dog's toys and discard any toy that starts to break into pieces or has pieces torn off.
- Toys that contain a "squeaker" or sound (like our toy) buried in its center may cause the dog to seek and destroy the sound source, and he could ingest it. These types of toys should be given only under supervision.
- For sizing, a toy should be small enough to carry around, and it should be the size that the prey would be for your dog.

IMPORTANT: Smooth Corners ·········

Do not draw any sharp edges, turns, or corners. These are more difficult to sew, and we don't want our "bad boy" getting his lips, gums, or tongue poked by a naughty point.

3. Lay the Toy Front on top of fabrics A and B, making sure A and B have their right sides together. Cut the fabric using the Toy Front as a guide. You now have backings for the Toy Front and Back.

4. Align the wrong side of the Toy Front to the right side of the Front Backing and sew a ¼" (6mm) seam. Remember this is a dog toy; therefore, all seams must be strong (B).

5. With the Toy's right sides together, sew the Front and Back pieces with a ½" (13mm) seam, leaving an opening large enough for your sound kit to go through. Turn the Toy right side out and press.

6. Topstitch ¼" (6mm) from the edge, avoiding the opening. Insert the sound kit, add cotton stuffing, and topstitch the opening closed (C).

✳ **TIP:** If your chosen fabrics are from your ex-boyfriend's left-behind outfits (you know you have those!), we suggest you try a monkey sound kit.

USE & CARE

>> Spot clean with a pet-safe cleaner. If you really want to machine wash it, remove the sound kit and stuffing beforehand.

>> To replace the battery, cut open the original opening to take out the sound kit.

↻ remix

• Design your own print and try your hand at screen-printing.

• Try out different sound kits.

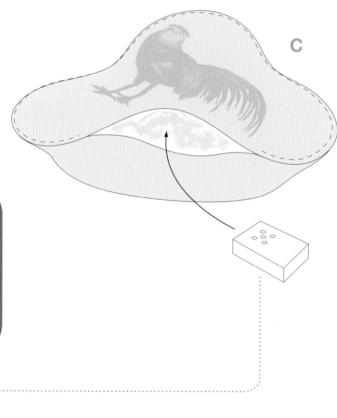

A PLUSH JINGLING CAT TOY

seafood cat toy

With a mild vibration, this stuffed toy will provide your kitty with hours of fun pouncing and stalking.
Now every modern kitty can have a wiggling and jingling feast of seafood any time of day.

seafood cat toy

[CRAFT] ■ □ □   [TECH] ■ ■ □   [COST] ■ ■ □

[MATERIALS & TOOLS]

FABRIC A, EXTERIOR: 6″ x 3½″ (15cm x 9cm) wool felt

FABRIC B, TENTACLES: 10″ x 8″ (25.5cm x 20.5cm) wool felt

FABRIC C, PUPILS: 2″ x 2″ (5cm x 5cm) black wool felt for the pupils

FABRIC D, EYES: 2″ x 2″ (5cm x 5cm) blue or

colored wool felt for around the eye

4″ (10cm) length of ½″ (13mm) wide sew-on Velcro

All-purpose thread in a matching color to fabric A

10″ (25.5cm) long piece of string or ribbon of your choice

Vibrating Motor Set (page 121)

Double-sided foam tape

Pushbutton switch (page 105)

Cotton stuffing

Optional: 2-3 small jingle bells

Core tools (page 106)

PATTERN (page 139)

1. Cut one Squid Front and one Squid Back from fabric A. Cut out seven Tentacles of varying lengths from fabric B. We used two 6″ (15cm) lengths, two 4½″ (11.4cm) lengths, two 5½″ (14cm) lengths, and one 4″ (10cm) length. Cut a Button Indicator from fabric B. Cut two Pupils from fabric C and two Eyes from fabric D.

2. With the wrong side up, arrange four Tentacles between the outside seam lines on the Squid Back. Pin one side of the Velcro over the Tentacles ⅛″ (3mm) down from the top of the Tentacles. Sew across the Squid Back, Velcro, and Tentacles as marked **(A)**. Repeat on the Squid Front with the other three Tentacles and the other side of the Velcro.

3. Hand-sew the string to the wrong side of the Squid Back, inside the seam allowance, as marked **(B)**.

4. With right sides facing and the string pulled around to the right side, sew the Front and Back together along the outside seams **(C)**. This is your Squid Body.

5. Turn right side out. Hand-sew the eyes, pupils, and Button Indicator as marked on the pattern.

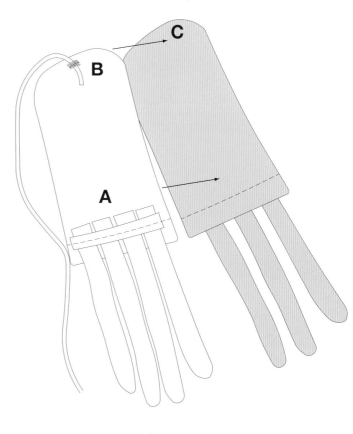

6. To create the vibration, refer to page 121 to make a Vibrating Motor Set with the pushbutton switch. Cut a piece of double-sided foam tape that fits the switch bottom, and apply one side of the tape to the switch bottom **(D)**. Insert the pack into the Squid Body **(E)**.

7. Place the switch button directly under the Button Indicator on the back and secure it to the wrong side of the Squid Front with the other side of the foam tape. For extra support, sew the switch wires to the Squid Back by creating two Xs around each wire **(F)**.

8. Stuff the body and close by fastening the Velcro.

9. Add one or more bells to the string near the top of the Squid.

↺ remix

- Come up with your own seafood design for the toy, such as jellyfish (as seen in the photos) or sushi.
- Add just a touch of catnip inside the toy to make it even more fun for your feline.
- Remove the bell(s) if your cat dislikes the jingles.

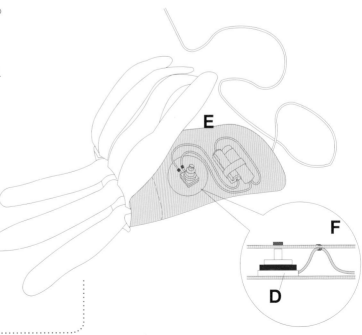

USE & CARE

>> Tie the string to a doorknob, a wall hook, or a piece of furniture.

>> Push the button to turn on the motor and watch it shimmy and shake with a jingling sound.

>> Replace the battery when the motion diminishes.

TALKING WII™
CARICATURE

mii doll

Now you can make a plush doll modeled after yourself, your loved ones, or your favorite celebrity. Equipped with a hidden audio recorder, the doll can deliver the person's favorite catch phrase or famous last words. You don't have to play games to love this doll.

[CRAFT] ■ ■ □   [TECH] ■ ▦ □   [COST] ■ ■ □

[MATERIALS & TOOLS]

FABRIC A, BODY: ½" yd (45.7cm) skin-colored cotton matching caricature's skin tone

FABRIC B, HAIR: ¼" yd (22.9cm) wool felt

FABRIC C, EYEBROWS: 2" x 2" (5cm x 5cm) wool felt

THREAD A: all-purpose silk or polyester thread of a matching color to fabric A

17½" (44.5cm) strip of ½" (13mm) wide sew-on Velcro

Tracing paper

Keychain audio recorder (page 35)

Ballpoint pen

Embroidery hoop, 7" (18cm) in diameter

Various embroidery floss colors: Black for the outlines of the nose, mouth, and eyes, and

colors that match eye color, lip color, and any beauty marks.

32" (81cm) 24-gauge wire

Cotton stuffing

Core tools (page 106)

PATTERN (page 135)

DESIGN THE CHARACTER

1. Decide who your "model" will be and visit one of the Mii design websites (we used http://www.miiware.com) to create his or her Mii avatar. When you are done, print out your Mii.

2. Adjust your printer settings to enlarge the face so that the eyes, nose, and mouth fit within the Front face pattern. Use your best judgment on the scale; you may have to do this several times before getting it right. If your face shape is different from our pattern, modify the face shape on the pattern to your liking before cutting.

3. Cut out the Front and Back from fabric A. Cut out two Back Heads, a Play Button, and a Record Button from fabric B. Trace the shapes of frontal hair and eyebrows onto fabrics B and C respectively, then cut out.

+ + IMPORTANT: Printing and Saving Your Mii Designs Every online Mii generator is different; please follow their instructions for printing. Alternatively, you may simply print out the webpage. Some sites also allow you to save your Mii characters, which is very helpful because it allows you more time to work and go back and manipulate the images.

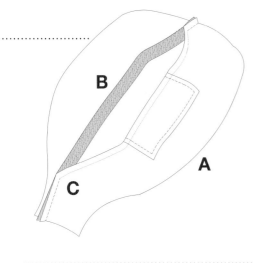

MAKE THE BACK

4. Create a patch pocket (page 109) that fits the recorder with a ½″ (13mm) seam allowance. Pin and sew the Recorder Pocket at the marks to the wrong side of a Back Head piece as indicated on the pattern **(A)**.

5. Cut a pair of 8¾″ (22cm) strips of Velcro, and sew one to the right side of each Back Head piece as marked **(B)**. Sew the two Back pieces with right sides together along the seam line, avoiding the Velcro **(C)**. Press the seam to wrong side.

6. With right sides together, sew the completed Back Head to the Back with a ¼″ (6mm) seam **(D)**.

mii: invasion of the virtual body snatchers

Miis are on-screen avatars created on Nintendo's popular Wii console. The idea is to design one after your own likeness, and use it as a character in Wii games. Of course, fans are not going to stop there.

They create more Miis for their family, friends, celebrities, and fictional characters. People share, compete, and even hold virtual parties for their Miis to mingle. As a species we seem very eager to recreate our experiences in the virtual world, where we can be free to try out different personas. Wii lovers now produce Mii T-shirts, wear Mii costumes, and even make Mii wedding cake toppers. It's all part of a larger trend that sees the blurring of physical and digital spaces. It is no wonder you picked up this book!

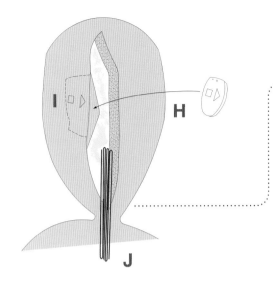

USE & CARE

>> Press the record button to record the person's voice, and the play button to hear the doll talk.

>> Take out the recorder to replace batteries. Refer to the manual for instructions.

>> Spot cleaning recommended.

CREATE THE FACE

7. Using tracing paper and a pointed edge, such as a pen, trace your printed Mii's face onto the wrong side of the Front piece. Stretch your facial area onto the embroidery hoop, and use a simple straight stitch to embroider the outlines of the eyes, nose, and mouth. Embroider the solid areas of the eyes, nose, mouth, and any facial markings, such as a mole, with the appropriate thread color **(E)**.

8. Sew on the frontal hair shape, and glue on the eyebrows and any optional accessories—glasses, for instance **(F)**.

9. With right sides together, sew the Front and Back pieces together with a ¼" (6mm) seam, leaving an opening at the top of the head **(G)**. Turn the doll right side out.

PUT IT ALL TOGETHER

10. After removing any chain, loop, or other attachments from the audio recorder, insert it into the pocket with the button side up **(H)**. Sew or glue the Play and Record Buttons to the Head Back, aligning them directly over the play and record buttons of the recorder **(I)**.

11. Fold the 24-gauge wire 3 times to make an 8" (20.5cm) rod. Place the wire inside the doll, centering it at the neck. This gives support to the doll's large head **(J)**. Stuff the doll.

12. Record the common expression or catchphrase of the real person after whom the doll is modeled on the recorder. Using fabric scraps or old clothes, make outfits for the doll based on the person's typical ensemble.

↻ remix

- Make a mini version that you can carry to your next Wii™ party.
- Design the look of your doll without using a Mii generator.

QUIVERS
WHEN PINNED

voodoodoll

Found in the depths of an ancient civilization, complete with magic spell, the vibrating VooDooDoll can be made in effigy of that no-good boss, the guy who stood you up last night, or anyone else on your not-so-nice list. Stick a pin in your victim and feel them wiggle and squirm right in your hands. Whether your revenge is sweet or not, it sure will be electrifying.

[CRAFT] ■ □ □   [TECH] ■ ■ □   [COST] ■ □ □

[MATERIALS & TOOLS]

FABRIC A, BODY: 14″ x 14″ (35.5cm x 35.5cm) medium-weight woven fabric, such as burlap or cotton (try an old sack with images on it)

4″ x 5″ (10cm x 12.5cm) foam, 3/4″ (2cm) thick

4″ x 5″ (10cm x 12.5cm) conductive fabric (page 104)

13″ (33cm) strip of 1/2″ (13mm) wide sew-on Velcro

All-purpose thread to match fabric A

Thread of your choice for the mouth

Two buttons of your choice for the eyes

Vibrating Motor Set (page 121)

Pincushion Switch (page 118)

Cotton stuffing

Stick pin longer than the thickness of your foam or sponge

Core tools (page 106)

PATTERN (page 138)

1. Cut out the Doll Front and Doll Back from fabric A. Cut out one Pincushion Switch piece from the foam and two from the conductive fabric.

2. Cut two 6½″ (16.5cm) strips of Velcro; sew them onto the two Doll Back pieces **(A)**.

3. Sew the two Doll Back pieces with right sides together as marked **(B)**.

4. On the right side of the Doll Front, create the mouth by embroidering several Xs and the eyes by sewing on two buttons **(C)**.

5. Sew the Doll Front and Doll Back together with right sides facing, using a 1/4″ (6mm) seam allowance **(D)**.

6. Make a Vibrating Motor Set (instructions on page 121).

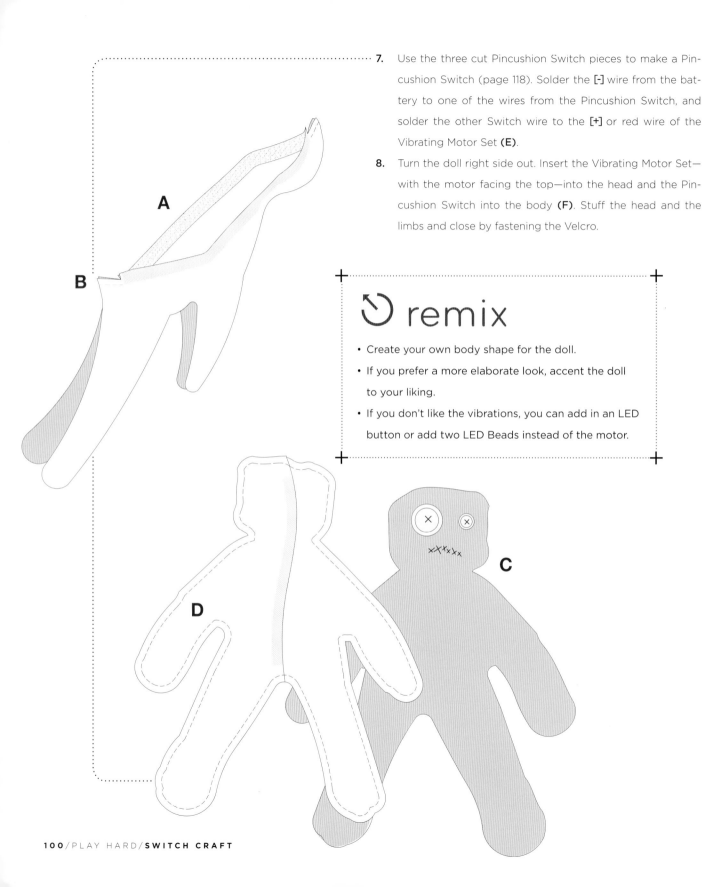

7. Use the three cut Pincushion Switch pieces to make a Pincushion Switch (page 118). Solder the [-] wire from the battery to one of the wires from the Pincushion Switch, and solder the other Switch wire to the [+] or red wire of the Vibrating Motor Set **(E)**.

8. Turn the doll right side out. Insert the Vibrating Motor Set—with the motor facing the top—into the head and the Pincushion Switch into the body **(F)**. Stuff the head and the limbs and close by fastening the Velcro.

↻ remix

- Create your own body shape for the doll.
- If you prefer a more elaborate look, accent the doll to your liking.
- If you don't like the vibrations, you can add in an LED button or add two LED Beads instead of the motor.

A

B

C

D

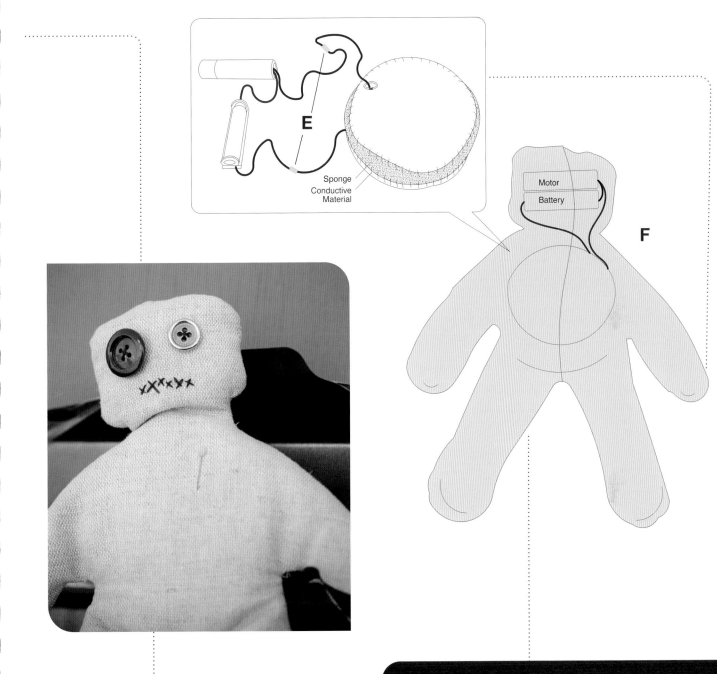

E

Sponge
Conductive
Material

F

Motor

Battery

USE & CARE

>> Stick a pin deep into the doll's body to trigger the vibration.

>> When the vibration weakens, change the battery.

>> Remove all electronic parts and stuffing before washing.

BASICS

BASIC SWITCH MATERIALS

Just as sewing requires a needle and thread, working with electronics requires some basic materials. We've compiled a list of these technologies, plus cool gadgets you'll be working with. If this seems very new to you, try to think of it like fabric notions. You may have fabric, but without the needle and thread to hold it together, you can't make anything. The same thing goes for electronics. You can't make something vibrate, light up, or make noise if you don't have a power source!

BATTERIES

Batteries are your power source: They give your project the energy it needs to run. The batteries used in this book are the standard AAA battery (1.5 volt), 9-volt battery, size 10 hearing-aid battery (1.4 volt), and a 3-volt coin cell battery, or just "coin battery." For the coin battery we recommend the CR2354, CR2450, or CR2430, in that order. Other batteries will be required for the electronic products incorporated into the projects. Since we can't predict which products you'll buy off-the-shelf, please read the manual for power requirement information for whatever product you're using.

BATTERY HOLDERS AND SNAPS

Both battery holders and snaps allow you to change the battery without affecting the circuit. The holder is a compartment into which you place the batteries and is designed for many different sizes and types of batteries (A). The Battery snap is not enclosed, and only works with the 9-volt battery. It has two snaps on top where you click the battery into place (B). For certain projects in this book, we have invented our own battery holders: Battery Snap Cap (page 116) and Skinny Power Pack (page 115). Still, a few projects require a commercially made 9-volt battery snap (A) or an AAA battery holder (B). You can find them at your local Radio Shack or from an online electronic component store. When purchasing a holder or snap, pick one with [+] and [–] wires already connected. Otherwise, you'll have to add the wires yourself.

> ⚠️ **CAUTION:** Although it might seem like a smart way to save money and time, never solder wires directly to a battery. It can be hazardous.

WIRE

Electric wire's job is to carry power or energy from one end to the other, and is used for connecting electronic components. It is essential for working with electronics, so Switch Crafters should always have some wire in their arsenal. When shopping for yours or opening up electronic products, you may encounter the following types of wire:

Types of Wire

solid-core wire (C) It consists of a solid wire wrapped inside a plastic coat.

stranded wire (D) Under its plastic coat you will see a bunch of fine-gauge wires instead of one thick wire as in the solid-core type. Therefore, the stranded wire is softer than the solid-core and also less breakable when twisted or bent.

magnet wire (E) Sometimes when you remove the coating of a cable, there are multiple stranded wires inside—each in a different color and twisted together without a coat. These colored wires are called magnet wires because of their applications

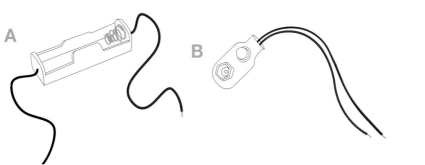

A   B   C   D

in electromagnetism, though the wires themselves are not magnetic. If you look carefully, you will notice that the "color" is actually a very thin layer of insulation.

coaxial cable (F)   There are many variations of coaxial cables. The one that you are likely to see when hacking a mobile headset or a speaker should look similar to our illustration: At its core is a solid or stranded wire with a coat, and surrounding it is a bundle of naked or magnet wires. Most people are more familiar with the solid core type, and we recommend it for its ease of use.

Buying Wire

Like thread or buttons, your wires needn't be dull. You can go for the standard electrical wires found at your hardware or electronics store, or make it extra colorful with jewelry wires:

standard electrical wires   Ask for 22-, 24-, or 26-gauge solid-core wire, and buy at least two different colors. The convention to use red wire for [+] and black wire for [–], so that they can always be distinguished easily. A low-cost and earth-friendly solution is to recycle wires from unused phone cords or Ethernet cables for a computer.

Carefully slice open the plastic jacket to get to the wires inside. Just note that these wires are usually quite thin and can be a bit more difficult to use.

jewelry wires   You should be able to find colorful coated wires for jewelry-making, such as the Fun Wire made by Toner, in your neighborhood craft store. **Beware that these wires are not sold for electronic applications.** Inspect each of your cut wire pieces to make sure that there is no crack or hole in the plastic coat before using them.

LEDS

Light-emitting diodes, or LEDs, are small, low cost, low-heat-dissipating, reliable lights found in almost every electronic product. Look around you: They indicate your VCR is on, blink when a battery is low, and light up everything from your cell phone to toys. These sparkling treasures come in endless sizes, shapes, and colors and light up when electricity is applied to their legs.

More specifically, the [+] side of your battery connects to the [+] leg of an LED, while the [–] side connects to the [–] leg. It's easy, but if you carelessly connect it in reverse, no electricity can go through and

your LED will not light up. For the aspiring technorati out there, this is called polarity. To learn how to distinguish the [+] from the [–], refer to the illustration (G).

In this book we use three different types of LEDs: a 5mm round LED, a 3mm round LED, and a surface-mount LED that is around $1æ/10''$ (3mm) in diameter on the top (H). The 3mm and 5mm LEDs look like domed crystal or acrylic beads with two long wires, called legs, while the surface-mount LED is the size of a tiny bead with no holes and silver on each side. When looking for surface-mount LEDs, remember that they are also called SMDs or SMT LEDs.

To find the right LED for your creation, you'll need to know the characteristics associated with LEDs so you will know what to look for. If you do not see this information on the LED or the package, it's often found in the product data sheet:

Typical Forward Voltage (Vf)

This refers to the most typical and efficient voltage it takes to light up an LED. It is around 3 volts for the 3mm and 5mm LEDs and around 3.5 volts for the surface-mount LED. Watch out, as the voltage rating (Vf) changes depending on the color

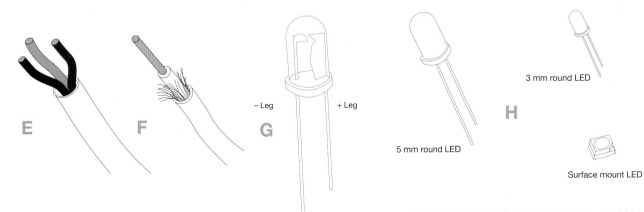

– Leg   + Leg

5 mm round LED

3 mm round LED

Surface mount LED

E   F   G   H

you choose. Reds and oranges require less voltage while blues require more.

Color of light

LEDs come in millions of colors. Be sure to get a color that looks good on your project (and on you, too).

Brightness

A higher mcd (millicandela, a unit of luminous intensity) number means a brighter LED. Dimmer ones usually help the battery last longer, while brighter ones are more eye-catching.

Viewing angle

This is the angle at which the light shines from the top of the LED. A wider angle (120–360 degrees) LED spreads the light better, while a narrower one (15–30 degrees) usually projects the light farther.

Special feature

Some LEDs blink or change colors. When used tastefully, they can add surprise and fun to your creation. However, make sure you buy those special LEDs with only two legs. Complex LEDs with more than 2 legs do not fall within the scope of this book.

⚠ **CAUTION:** Usually, people use something called a resistor between the LED light and the power source to prevent too much electric current from going to the LED and burning it out. We've taken out the guesswork and provided the correct voltage to the correct LED in each project, so you don't need a resistor if you follow the guidelines and materials lists correctly.

Here are some basic LED rules to follow:

• If you don't know the specifications of an LED, it's better not to use it.

• Do not use an LED with a Vf rating much lower than the suggested values above. The LED may still work, but it will generate more heat and thus decrease its lifespan. If you do use an LED with a much lower Vf rating, do not leave your LED on for long periods of time.

• If the Vf rating is much higher than our suggestions, the LED may not light up at all, so stick to our guidelines.

CONDUCTIVE FABRICS AND THREAD

Conductive fabric and thread have similar properties to electrical wire, just different forms. It may sound like top secret NASA stuff, but it's easier to find than you may think. Fencers have been wearing lamés—jackets made of conductive fabric—for scoring purposes for some time. Lately, people working in the fashion technology field have rediscovered conductive fabrics and thread as a way to add interactivity into their products, like iPod-controlling ski jackets. With conductive fabric or thread, you too can add the spice of electricity to your sewing crafts without the hard edges of wire. You can buy spools of conductive thread from an online lamé repair store or a local fencing supply vendor. We've found that online sellers of EMF (electromagnetic field) protection gear are likely to carry conductive fabric and thread, too. We've used Lamé Lifesavers (http://members.shaw.ca/ubik/thread/thread.html) and LessEMF (http://www.lessemf.com/fabric.html). You may also get lucky and find silk metallic organza in a fabric store. Visit our website to get tips on how to use the organza.

Please be mindful that conductive fabric and thread are the same as using uncoated electric wire or a metallic surface without insulation. Make sure you do not inadvertently cause any short circuits! There are many different fabrics with various textures, looks, and conductivity. LessEMF.com offers a conductive fabric sample kit. You may want to pick one up to identify the right fabric for your project. We picked the Zelt fabric for our VooDooDoll (page 98) and Pillow Talk (page 42) projects.

SWITCHES

At Switch, we like to make our own switches (see page 118 for the Pincushion Switch and page 119 for the Donut Switch). However, there are times when it is more fitting to utilize ready-made products. In this book you will come upon four types:

Slide switch

Slide switches are used in just about every electronic toy, and it's time for you to put it to work. Visit your local Radio Shack or online electronic component store for the SPST slide switch. (SPST basically means a single set of on-off controls.) We prefer smaller ones with mounting ears (A).

Pushbutton switch

This is another type of switch that we encounter daily. For the Seafood Cat Toy (page 91) you need an SPST off-on or on-off switch. These stay on with the first click and off with the second. Find one that is as short in height as possible if you want the toy to look slim—visit our website for recommendations. Do not buy a momentary switch that turns itself back on or off as soon as you lift your finger.

Reed switch

It looks like a long glass bead with two metal legs sticking out from both sides but is actually a switch, too. What's great about the reed switch is that you can apply a magnet to turn it on and remove the magnet to turn it off. Most electronic component stores sell them. Again, smaller ones get our vote (B). Make sure not to buy a "mercury" or "wetted" reed switch, because they contain mercury.

Magnetic switch

These switches are often used to detect the opening and closing of a door or window. They can be found in most local or online security equipment shops, hardware stores, and electronic component vendors that sell do-it-yourself security products. The switch consists of two halves: One is pre-wired, or has metal contacts for you to attach your own wires (you may have to remove a cap to see the contacts); the other half cannot be wired (C). When shopping, look for a switch that turns the circuit "on" when the two halves are apart; this is called the normally-closed type (NC). Some switches contain both NC and NO (normally-open) contacts; that, of course, will work too, as long as you use the NC part of it. And yes, purchase a miniature version if you can find one.

> ✳ **TIP:** In *Switch Craft*, we only use the switches listed or make our own, but there are actually millions of switches out there in every size, shape, color, texture, and action. Explore the world around you and find which ones you like and put them into your own creations.

HEAT SHRINK TUBING

Heat shrink tubing works like the heat shrink-wrap you find at craft stores. It is plastic tubing that shrinks in diameter when heat is applied. In electronics it's used to insulate objects, such as wires: You place wires in the tube and shrink it to protect and hold them tight. You can find the tubing in hardware stores and Radio Shack. Visit online vendors of electronic components, such as Jameco.com, for the best selection of sizes.

EL WIRE AND DRIVER

Electroluminescent (EL) wire is a thin rope that glows when electricity is applied. It's like being able to work with a string of light, and is often used to add a lined neon glow in costuming and decoration. What's

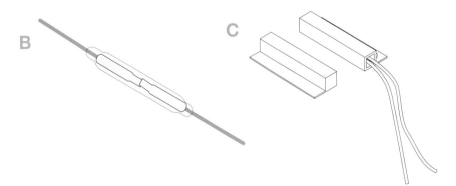

A

Body
Terminals

Mounting ears

B

C

even better is that EL wire is easy to use, flexible, cool to the touch, and comes in many colors and thicknesses. To power EL wire you'll need something called a driver, also known as an inverter. The inverter converts the DC (direct current) power from the battery to the AC (alternating current) power required by the EL wire. The power is determined by the length and diameter of your wire. There are many different kinds of drivers available. We have picked the following two types for Switch Crafters to use:

Portable/Hand Held Driver for Two AA Batteries

There should be a switch on the driver to turn the light on and off. Some drivers may feature a flashing mode, too (not required). Pick one with the smallest dimensions that you can find that powers the length of your EL wire. We picked one capable of powering at least 6' (1.8m) of 5mm EL wire in Cushion Brite (page 12). If a belt clip is included, remove it to reduce the size (A).

"Pipsqueak" or "Mini" Driver for a 9-Volt Battery

There should be no switch on the pipsqueak driver. Pick one with the smallest dimensions you can find, but make sure it is capable of powering at least 10' (3m) of 3mm EL wire or the appropriate length of your wire (B).

EL wire needs a special connector or "clasp" that connects it to the driver. We suggest you **buy wires with the connector attached**. If you can't find one or want a little challenge, you can attach it yourself following the instructions in the manual or on the vendor's website. The driver also requires a connector (C), and it is usually sold with one pre-attached; if not, you have to do that yourself as well. Both the wire and the driver can be easily bought from many online stores that specialize in EL products.

⚠ CAUTION: Do not apply power to your driver unless it is connected to an EL wire. The driver can be damaged if you do so. Also, keep in mind that EL wire won't work if exposed to excessive moisture.

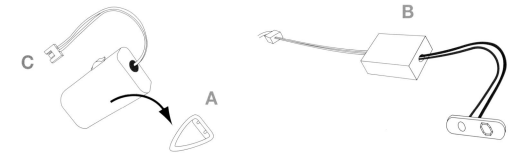

BASIC SWITCH TOOLS

CORE TOOLS—CRAFT

• sewing machine

Use a sewing machine you are familiar with. It needs to be large enough to work with a skirt or large pillow and perform all of the basic stitches, including zigzag and backstitch.

• fabric marking tools

Your tool can be a pen or chalk, or tracing paper and a tracing wheel. The type of fabric you use will determine which marking tool is best. As with everything, read the directions before using the marking tool on your fabric or test in an inconspicuous area.

✴ TIP: Always use the correct scissors for the correct application. Use fabric scissors on fabric and paper scissors on paper. It's a good idea to mark the fabric scissors with a piece of tape around the handle.

- **gripper snap tool**

It is used to attach gripper snaps to fabric and can be found in the fastening section of fabric stores. See page 111 for more info.

- **fabric or quilting ruler**

These rulers are transparent plastic so that you can see the fabric underneath.

- **fabric scissors, large and small**
- **paper scissors**
- **glue gun and hot glue**
- **fine point permanent marker**
- **jewelry pliers with rounded nose**
- **fabric tape measure**
- **no-sew fusible hemming tape**
- **fabric glue**
- **Fray Check liquid seam sealant**
- **straight pins**
- **embroidery needles**
- **hand-sewing needles**
- **seam ripper**
- **thimble**

CORE TOOLS—HARDWARE

- **soldering iron**

Soldering irons are used to heat up the solder to liquid form so that you can attach it to metal in a process called soldering (page 111). Purchase a 25-watt and up soldering iron with a fine-tipped point **(A)**. You can find a good soldering iron at any local craft or electronics store. You may already be familiar with the soldering guns used in stained-glass crafts. It is the same concept, but **do not** use a soldering gun for the projects in this book. They have a high wattage and use an electrical current to generate the heat. This is not a safe choice for electronics.

When selecting your soldering iron, please keep in mind that this is a crucial tool. A good one makes soldering easier and shields heat from your hand better. We suggest you buy a quality one in your price range. For those who plan to do a lot of soldering work, a soldering station with temperature control is a good investment **(B)**.

- **tip-cleaning tools**

There are two choices for keeping the tip of your soldering iron clean:

- **damp sponge** Many soldering irons come with a small sponge. Moisten the sponge with clean water (do not soak) and wipe the tip clean before and after each time you solder. If your iron didn't come with a sponge, you can purchase one or cut up one of your plain kitchen sponges. Replace it when it gets too dirty.

- **tip cleaner** Unlike the sponge, tip cleaner requires no water. Since sponges need frequent replacement and their use drops the tip's temperature, some people prefer tip cleaner. It looks like steel wool sitting inside a pad. Clean your tip by dipping—not wiping—it into the tip cleaner. Do not try to save money by using regular steel wool. It will destroy the tip.

- **solder (20–24 gauge)**

Solder looks like wire, but it is actually a metal alloy with a low melting point so that it can be heated up into a liquid blob with the soldering iron to bond metal objects together. It also allows electricity to pass through these bonded objects. The most common commercial solder is of the rosin-core variety, but we suggest you purchase lead-free solder for safety. Check the safety information on page 8 for more information.

A

B

• wire stripper

Wire strippers are used to tear off the plastic coating around wires. They come in two main varieties, the multiple-notch (C) and the single-notch (D). Refer to page 109 for illustrations and use directions.

• wire cutter

Most wire strippers have blades for cutting wires. However, if for some reason yours doesn't, buy a simple wire cutter from a hardware or craft store for the job.

• "third hand" clamps

These are great little gadgets that give you a helping hand by securely holding a part of your project, thus freeing up your hands for other work. They have two or three adjustable clamps and often a magnifying glass for doing delicate construction (E). Third hands are also called helping hands, and can be easily found in local hobby, jewelry, or craft supply shops.

• multimeter

A multimeter looks like a crazy kitchen timer, but it's actually an electronic measuring tool. It usually has a large knob in the center with electronic symbols all around it, a display window, and at least two wired prongs in red and black (F). They are found at your local hardware and electronic stores and come in a wide variety of prices and sizes, but don't let the store clerks oversell you on one with a million extras. For *Switch Craft,* we suggest a small digital model for around $10–$30.

• screwdrivers

These include flathead, Phillips, and a jeweler's/watchmaker's mini screwdriver set (flathead and Phillips).

• electrical tape

Available in many colors and sizes. We usually go with ½" (13mm) width.

- **X-Acto knife or utility knife**
- **needle-nose pliers**
- **regular gripping pliers**

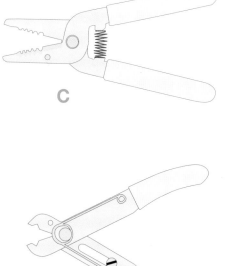

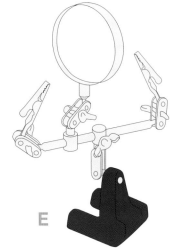

MAKING A PATCH POCKET

This technique is referenced frequently in the book for creating a customized fabric pocket for a gadget such as an MP3 player or cell phone. You can also use this technique to create a gadget holder for any purchased or pre-crafted item in your wardrobe. Make it from your project fabric and sew it onto the exterior or the lining. It's very easy to sew; just follow these steps:

1. Have the fabric piece for making the pocket cut and ready. If the size of the pocket is not given in your project's pattern or instructions, you need to first determine the dimensions. Measure your gadget's width, height, and depth and use the equations below to find your pocket size, and cut it out.

POCKET WIDTH = 2 DEPTHS + 1 WIDTH + 2 SEAM ALLOWANCES

POCKET HEIGHT = 1 DEPTH + 1 HEIGHT + $\frac{1}{4}$" (6MM)

2. Fold the side and bottom seam allowances to the wrong side and press with the iron to make a crease. Flip the pocket right side up, make a diagonal fold in the turned-back seam allowances at the corners, and press with the iron to create another crease.

3. Sew each diagonal crease you just made (A) and snip off the excess fabric (B).

4. Turn the pocket right side up and fold the sides and bottom seam allowances to the wrong side (C).

5. Fold the top edge of the pocket down $\frac{1}{4}$" (6mm) toward the wrong side and topstitch. Then, fold the top seam allowance under to the wrong side, press, and topstitch down (D).

6. Attach the pocket to your project by topstitching it to the location indicated on the pattern or in the instructions.

TIP: An alternative to sewing the seam allowances is to use a no-sew fusible tape, such as Stitch Witchery, to fuse the seam allowance to the wrong side of the pocket fabric. Fusible tape can be found at any fabric store, and each brand is different, so if you try this method be sure to read the product's directions.

STRIPPING WIRE

Virtually all the electrical wires that you are going to encounter when Switch Crafting will come wrapped in plastic coating to prevent short circuits. Before the wire can be used or soldered, you must strip away the insulation at its tip. Below we list a number of ways to strip your wires, depending on the type of wire (page 102) and wire stripper you have.

For Coated Solid-core or Stranded Wire

1. Decide how long you want the exposed wire tip to be. It depends on the situation, but we usually go with $\frac{1}{2}$" (13mm).

2. Determine the diameter of the metal

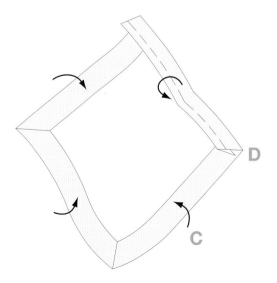

wire under the coat if you don't know the spec. You may simply estimate it or cut the wire to see the core.

3. Multiple-notch wire stripper only: If you have a wire stripper with multiple notches of varying sizes, open it and place your wire in the notch of the size that is about the same or slightly larger than the diameter of the wire under the coat, leaving what will become the exposed wire tip on the other side. Close the wire stripper firmly in one hand while holding the wire in the other. Pull the wire stripper out to the opposite side to remove the insulation.

4. Single-notch wire stripper only: If there is only one notch on your wire stripper, you can adjust the size of the notch by moving the nut and bolt combo on one of the blades (A). Make sure the notch is about the size of the diameter of the wire under the coat when the wire stripper is closed. Once you get the right size, open the stripper and place the wire in the notch, leaving what will become the exposed wire tip on the other side. Close the wire stripper firmly in one hand while holding the wire in the other. With a quick upward flip of the wrist, pull the wire stripper out to the opposite side to remove the insulation.

5. Wire cutter only: If you don't have a wire stripper on hand, a temporary solution is to use a wire cutter. Open the wire cutter and place your wire on one of the blades, leaving what will be the exposed tip on the other side. Carefully close the cutter to cut into the coat, making sure the blades do not cut into the wire underneath. Open the blades, rotate the wire 90 degrees, and close again. Use this method to cut a ring around the insulation and remove the coat by pulling it out by hand.

For Magnet Wire

1. Decide how long you want the exposed wire tip to be. It depends on the situation, but we usually go with $1/2$" (13mm).

2. If you are dealing with one stranded magnet wire, skip this step. If yours is a cable that contains multiple stranded magnet wires, slice open the cable jacket to reveal the inner wires.

3. Take one stranded magnet wire and untwist its tip. The tip now becomes a bunch of fine-gauge wires (B).

4. The "color" on every one of these fine-gauge wires is actually a thin layer of coat. Scratch the coat off with sandpaper or a nail file. Since there are so many wires, you don't have to get to every single one. Just do a decent job to expose the majority of them.

5. Twist the tiny wires back together into one stranded wire. If you are dealing with only one stranded magnet wire to begin with, stop here.

6. Do the same to the rest of the stranded magnet wires inside your cable.

For Coaxial Cable

1. Please note that these steps apply only to coaxial cable that consists of one coated solid-core or stranded wire at the center surrounded by a bundle of naked or magnet wires.

2. Decide how long you want the exposed wire tip to be. It depends on the situation, but we usually go with $1/2$" (13mm).

3. Slice open the cable jacket with a utility knife to reveal the inner wires. Separate the bundle of fine-gauge wires away from the coated wire (C).

4. To strip the wire in the middle, follow the instructions for coated solid-core or stranded wire.

5. If the fine-gauge wires look colorful, they are likely magnet wires. Follow the instructions for magnet wires to strip them. Then, twist them together to form a stranded wire (D).

6. If the fine-gauge wires are naked (without coating), just twist them together to form a stranded wire.

ATTACHING CONDUCTIVE THREAD OR WIRE TO GRIPPER SNAPS

When adding electronics to sewing projects, one of the main challenges is that wires can't be easily connected to fabric.

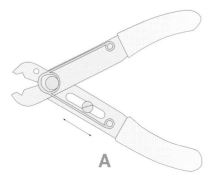

A   B   C   D

Our solution is to use the common gripper snap, found in fabric stores, to affix a wire or conductive thread to a piece of fabric. A pair of gripper snaps consists of male and female snaps:

- A male gripper snap includes a stud and a prong ring. The prong ring has five to six sharp pointers on the front that perforate through the fabric and attach to the stud on the other side to connect it to the fabric.
- A female gripper snap includes a socket and also a prong ring to connect it to the fabric.

Have your size 16 or 19 gripper snaps and your gripper snap tool ready. Below are the instructions on how to attach conductive thread or wire to a snap. Choose one based on what project you are making.

Attaching Conductive Thread (A)

1. Tightly wrap the end of your thread around the prong ring 2–3 times, and tie it off. Now read the instructions of your project carefully: If the snap is supposed to be fastened to a fabric piece, continue to step 2. If not, skip to step 3.

2. Place the prong ring on your fabric where marked. Make sure it is placed on the correct side based on your project instructions. Place either the stud or the socket (also depending on project directions) on the opposite side of your fabric.

3. Use your gripper snap tool to attach the prong ring per the tool's instructions to either the stud or the socket. Secure the thread and knot with hot glue or fabric glue as directed in the project instructions.

Attaching Wire (B)

1. Tightly wrap the stripped portion of your wire around the prong ring 2 times.

2. While using your "third hand" clamps (page 108) to hold the prong ring steady, solder the wire and the ring together on the non-pointy side of the ring. Only use a small amount of solder to avoid any clump on the pointy side of the ring. You want it neat and clean so that the wire and the solder will not get in the way later when attaching the prong ring to the gripper snap front.

3. Read the instructions for your project carefully: If the snap is supposed to be fastened to a fabric piece, continue to the next step. If not, skip to step 5.

4. Place the prong ring on your fabric where marked. Make sure it is placed on the correct side based on the project's instructions. Place either the stud or the socket (also depending on the instructions) on the opposite side of your fabric.

5. Use your gripper snap tool to attach the prong ring per the tool's instructions. Secure the solder joint with hot glue.

SOLDERING

Soldering (the "L" is silent) is what holds two pieces of metal or wire together. The soldering that you have to do for Switch Crafting is not too dissimilar to the soldering work for jewelry-making. Nonetheless, the focus here is to make the solder joints durable for daily use and clean for good conductivity. There are many books and online instructions available on this subject, and you may find them helpful. Don't be discouraged if you don't get it right the first time. The key is to practice, practice, practice! You will soon become a maestro.

CAUTION: As we mentioned earlier, do not inhale the fumes! Make sure the ventilation is good at your work space.

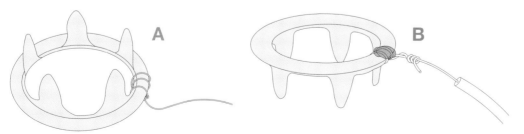

1. When soldering two wires, twist their tips together. If one of the wires is a lot softer and/or slimmer than the other, twist the softer/slimmer wire tip around the harder/larger one (A). If the objects are one wire and one metal plate, bend the tip of the wire slightly so that it can sit flat on the metal surface (B).

2. Use your "third hand" clamps (page 108) to hold the two objects steady and at an angle that is easy for you to solder (C). Turn on the soldering iron if you haven't done so, and wait for it to heat up.

3. Cut a piece of solder—length depends on how many joints you are soldering. We start at least 3" (7.5cm). When in doubt, err on the long side. Now pick up your soldering iron in one hand and hold the piece of solder in the other at the far end of the solder (or hold it with needle-nose pliers if you want to be safer).

4. Keep the soldering iron tip clean by dipping it in a tip cleaner or wiping it on a damp sponge. You will need to do this before and after soldering each joint to ensure clean solder joints.

✳ **TIP:** A clean soldering joint is shiny. Dull color is a telltale sign of a "dirty" joint.

5. Apply the soldering iron tip to the area where the two objects meet (D). Gradually heat up the area with the hot tip using long brushstroke-like motions. Do not dab at the solder. You may also need to heat up the back side of the area. Please note that if the object to be soldered is an electronic component, such as an LED, be careful not to overheat it.

6. Station the soldering iron tip at the exact location where you want the joint to be, and place the end of the solder at the seam—not

on the soldering iron tip—between the soldering iron tip and the underlying objects (E). The solder should melt instantly. Push in more solder (moderately) if you want the liquid blob to grow; pull out to stop.

7. You have a very short window of time in which to guide or shape the blob before it solidifies—act fast but delicately! When done, swiftly withdraw the soldering iron. You may blow air onto the newly made joint to accelerate the cool down.

8. Examine the joint to see if you have to strengthen it by adding more solder to the joint or to its back side.

✳ **TIP:** If you make a bad joint that is beyond repair, cut the wire and start again, or desolder the joint. Desoldering instructions can be found on many websites, such as the Electronics Club (www.kpsec.freeuk.com).

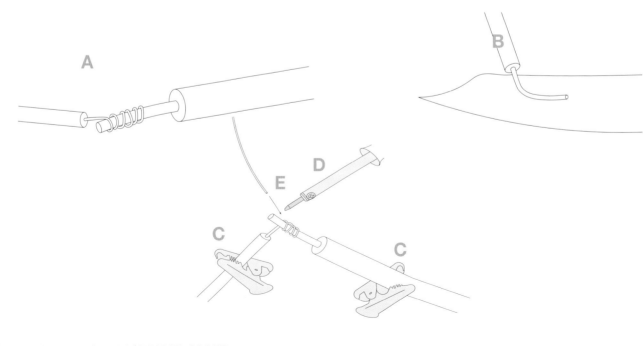

INSULATING WIRE

Again, we'd like to remind you of the importance of short-circuit prevention. To keep the [+] and [−] wires from touching, it is always a good idea to insulate them. You can insulate exposed wires and contacts by one of the following means:

- Hot glue (A)
- Electrical tape (B)
- Heat shrink tubing (C)

In this book we focus on the first two insulation methods, since they may be more familiar to you. However, should you want to try the shrink tube, read the descriptions on page 105 and also do an online search for instructions.

USING A MULTIMETER

Unlike sewing or most other crafting work, you can't naturally see if something is hooked up or working properly in electronic handiwork. Even an impeccable-looking solder joint might not conduct electricity effectively from one wire to the other. Therefore, we recommend you test your circuit after each step that involves any electronic component with a multimeter (page 108), sold at hardware stores and electronics stores. It is also helpful for troubleshooting during the construction of a project or after it is made and used. For the purposes of this book, you'll have to learn how to test voltage and continuity with your multimeter.

Testing Voltage

In many cases, a nonworking circuit is caused by a depleted power source. If your electronic creation is not working, before you tear it apart to search for faulty connections, make sure there is enough juice in your battery or battery pack. Even brand new batteries could be DOA—so do check. Here's how:

1. Place your battery or battery pack (page 115) on a nonconductive surface such as wood. Secure its position so that it won't roll around. Use "third hand" clamps if needed.

2. Set your multimeter to voltage-testing mode. Consult the manual if you don't know how.

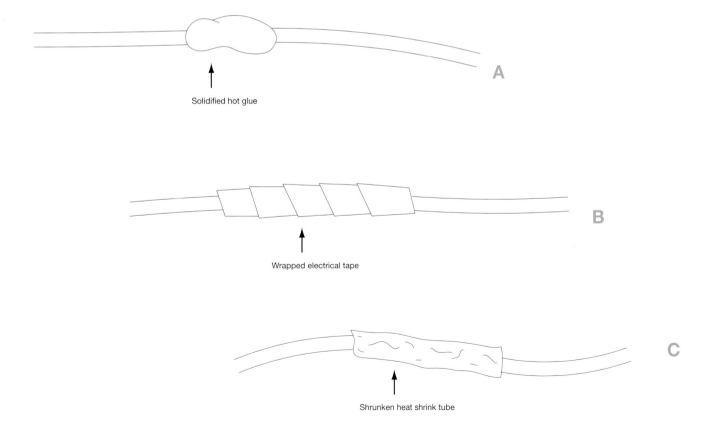

Solidified hot glue

A

Wrapped electrical tape

B

Shrunken heat shrink tube

C

3. Hold one probe in each hand. Simultaneously touch the **[+]** and **[−]** contacts on your battery with the red and black probe tips respectively, and hold steady **(A)**. You should now see a reading of voltage on the multimeter's display.

4. If the number is much lower than the voltage rating on the tested battery's casing (AAA is 1.5 volts; a 9-volt battery is, well, 9 volts), it's time to replace it. For the expected voltage reading for a serial battery configuration such as the Skinny Power Pack, refer to page 116.

Testing Continuity

Loose connections and badly soldered joints are the bane of Switch Crafters because a constant flow of electricity is essential for any electronic circuit to be operational. Whenever you tie or sew a piece of conductive thread to another piece or to a metallic object, or solder two things together, you want to be sure that the connection is good. Use a multimeter to check the continuity:

1. Place the connected objects on a non-conductive surface. Secure their positions so that they won't move around easily. Use "third hand" clamps if needed.

2. Set your multimeter to continuity-testing mode. Consult the manual if you don't know how.

3. Hold one probe in each hand. Identify two points (on metallic or conductive fabric, not on plastic coating) on opposite sides of the joint. Simultaneously touch these two points with the two probe tips, and hold steady **(B)**.

4. For most multimeters, if the connection is good, you should hear a continuous beep. If there is no sound or the sound is intermittent, the connection is most likely loose and needs to be fixed. Not all multimeters make a sound, so please consult your manual.

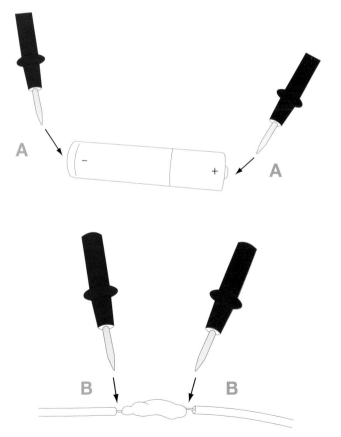

OR

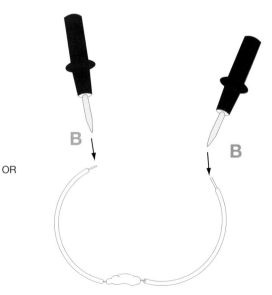

BASIC SWITCH ELEMENTS

SKINNY POWER PACK

Based on the size 10 hearing-aid battery, the Skinny Power Pack is compact and lightweight. We have created two variations: the quick-change version for quicker battery pack replacement, and the secure version for tighter connection and insulation. Either one is equally good for your projects, except the Petit Four D-Light (page 38), for which the secure version is required.

[MATERIALS & TOOLS]

Size 10 hearing-aid batteries: refer to the materials list of your project for the number of batteries to use

Heat shrink tubing: one tube of 5mm inside diameter and one tube of 6mm inside diameter; each 1½" (3.8cm) long

Heat gun or hairdryer

A pair of magnetic jewelry clasps

Core tools (page 106)

IMPORTANT: Magnetic Clasps
We recommend the typical magnetic clasps you find in jewelry making supply stores for necklaces or bracelets. You'll need to test which size fits best into your shrink tube. The only requirement is that the contact surfaces on both sides must be flat; do not buy a pair with male-female contacts. We've also found that a thicker cylinder-like clasp works better than a slender cone-like shape.

Quick-Change Version

1. Refer to the instructions for your project for the number of batteries to use. As illustrated, stuff them into a shrink tube of 5mm diameter, stacking them together as closely as possible, one on top of the other. It's OK for **[+]** and **[-]** to touch in this instance. Cut off the excess tubing, leaving only ¹⁄₁₆" (1.5mm) extra on both sides **(A)**.

2. Test the voltage with a multimeter. Touch the two ends of the battery stack with the multimeter probes. You should see about 1.4 volts for every battery in the pack. If your reading is much lower, one or more batteries may not be fresh or they are not stacked together tightly enough. Make note of which side is **[+]** and which is **[-]**.

3. Carefully use a heat gun or hairdryer to shrink the tube. To prevent overheating, do it in a quick, continuous left-right panning motion and keep it at least 1' (30.5cm) away from the tube. Turn the hair dryer off frequently for short breaks to let the batteries cool down. Stop when you see that the tube has shrunk enough to hold the batteries firmly.

CAUTION: For your safety, never overheat a battery.

4. On the tube, mark the **[+]** and **[-]** sides of the batteries using a permanent marker. Since the hearing-aid battery (a.k.a. the zinc-air battery) needs oxygen to generate electricity, poke a few pinholes with a straight pin into the casing between batteries to let air in **(B)**.

5. Insert the shrunken tube into the 6mm diameter tube. Measure the length of your magnetic clasp. Cut the wider tube while leaving the length of the clasp on each ends **(C)**.

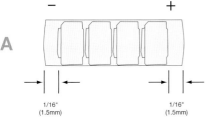

A

−   +

1/16"
(1.5mm)

1/16"
(1.5mm)

B

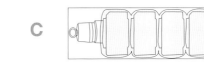

C

Secure Version

1. Measure the length of your magnetic clasp. Refer to the instructions of your current project for the number of batteries to use. Stuff them into a shrink tube of 5mm diameter. Make sure the batteries are stacked together as closely as possible. Cut off the excess tubing, leaving the length of the clasp—plus 1/16" (1.5mm) extra—on each end. Insert the clasps into the tube as illustrated (A).

2. Test the voltage by touching the two clasps with the multimeter probes. See step 2 of the quick-change version for details.

3. Follow steps 3 and 4 of the quick-change version to complete your battery pack. The only difference is that the clasps are now wrapped in the shrunken tube (B).

IMPORTANT: Serial Battery Configuration When multiple batteries are connected together end-to-end with one battery's [+] touching the next battery's [–], they effectively become one battery with higher voltage. This is called a serial connection. For example, the combined voltage of three 1.4 volt batteries connected serially is 4.2 volts (1.4 + 1.4 + 1.4).

BATTERY SNAP CAP

The Battery Snap Cap is an easily made snap-in/snap-out battery holder for 3-volt coin batteries.

[MATERIALS & TOOLS]

Gripper snaps, one socket and one stud, size 16 or 19

2 prong rings

Felt tip marker

3-volt coin battery (page 102)

Core tools (page 106)

Plastic key cap or key cover

TIP: As tempting as it may be to order those Hello Kitty® key caps sold on the Internet, do not buy key caps online. Go to a local hardware store and find one that will hold your battery snugly.

1. Using the gripper snap tool, crimp together the prong ring and stud (male) gripper snap to one side of the plastic key cover with the prong ring on the interior. Use the same technique for the socket (female) gripper snap on the other side of the plastic key cover (C).

2. Mark a [+] sign on the side of the plastic key cover with the stud and mark a [–] sign on the side of the plastic key cover with the socket (D).

3. Put in your 3-volt battery and make sure to align the [+] and [–] sides of the battery with the [+] and [–] sides of the plastic key cover (E).

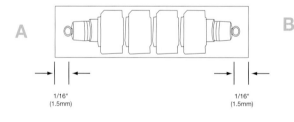

A

1/16"
(1.5mm)   1/16"
(1.5mm)

B

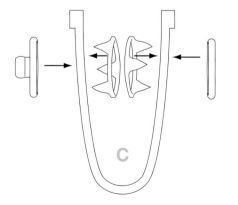

C

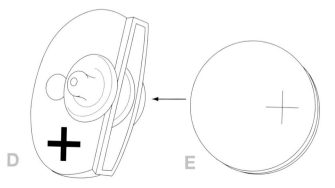

D

E

4. When inside, your battery should be in contact with the backs of both of the prong rings. Test the voltage coming from the snaps to ensure your voltage equals the voltage of your battery. It should be around 3.1 volts. If the voltage is much lower, your battery may be dead or it may not be hitting the contacts. Double check the battery and ensure good contact.

5. Once the reading is accurate, you are ready to snap the power into your project.

6. To replace the battery, simply remove it from the plastic key cover and put in a new battery.

LED BUTTON AND REFLECTIVE CONE

The LED Button is used to add sparkle and light to your creation. It's made with familiar materials like a button and duct tape, which provide a sturdy base for your LED. For some of the projects, such as the Aromatherapy Sachet (page 82), we rec-ommend that you add a Reflective Cone to the Button to enhance its brightness

[MATERIALS & TOOLS]

One or three 3mm or 5mm LEDs: Refer to the materials list of your project for the number and type of LEDs to use

One 2-hole button for the one-LED setup or one 4-hole button for use with three LEDs, about ³⁄₄" (2cm) in diameter, the thinner the better, with a raised outside edge

Reflective cone only: Polyester film (such as reflective Mylar) or foil; refer to the materials list of your project for the size

Reflective cone only: 2" (5cm) wide duct tape

Core tools (page 106)

....

LED Button with One LED

1. Put the **[–]** leg of your LED in one hole of the button and the **[+]** leg in the oppo-site hole as shown (A). Mark the **[+]** and **[–]** on the bottom side of the button with a permanent marker.

2. Use pliers to bend each LED leg around the bottom side of the button, leaving just a bit of space for wire connection later (B). Wrap each leg back onto the top, clip it to the raised edge of the button closely for support, and cut off the excess (C).

LED Button with Three LEDs

1. Insert the three LEDs into the button as illustrated (D). As you can see, two of the button holes each have two LED legs in them. Twist two legs together as shown.

2. Follow step 2 of the one-LED version to wrap the legs of your LEDs around the button. Make sure the bottom of your but-ton looks like our illustration (E). Use a permanent marker to write **[+]** and **[–]** on the button to indicate the beginning **[+]** leg and the ending **[–]** leg (not the twisted legs).

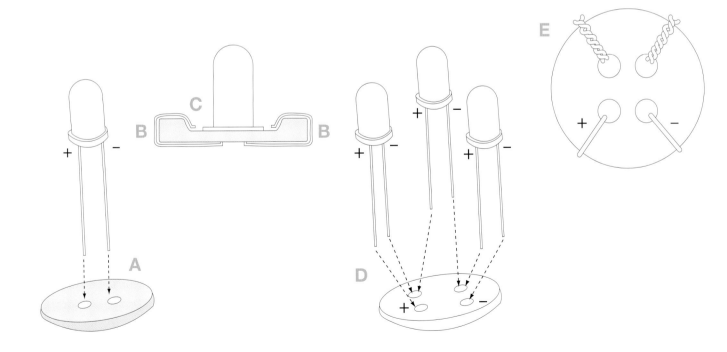

Reflective Cone

1. Take your piece of Mylar or foil and attach duct tape to the back for stability. Cut it into a 3" (7.5cm) circle and cut a small circular hole in the center that is just large enough to surround the LED(s), but not as big as the button attached to the LED. Slice a line on one side from the outside edge to the central hole **(A)**.

2. Adjust the Mylar into a cone shape around the LED(s) and duct tape the cone closed **(B)**. Secure the cone to your LED button using hot glue.

PINCUSHION SWITCH

There is nothing like the Pincushion Switch. Stick a pin in it and it can make your project light up or quiver, like in the VooDooDoll (page 98). It's a section of foam or sponge sandwiched between two pieces of conductive fabric. When you stick a pin through the switch it connects the two pieces of conductive fabric.

[MATERIALS & TOOLS]

Sponge or foam (type and size is indicated in the
  project's materials list—not a kitchen sponge)
Conductive fabric (size indicated in the materials
  list)
Electrical wire
Gripper snaps, 2 sockets size 16 or 19
2 prong rings
Solder
All-purpose thread in any color
Straight pin longer than the thickness of your foam
  or sponge
Core tools (page 106)

....

1. Cut two pieces of conductive fabric and the foam/sponge into the shape indicated by the project pattern or directions.

2. Cut two 7" (18cm) lengths of wire and strip both ends. Then, follow the instructions on page 111 for soldering one wire to each gripper snap prong ring.

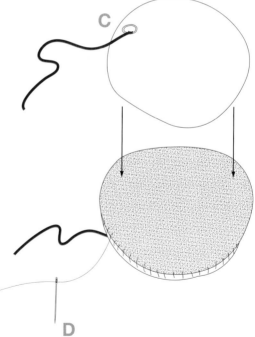

3. Next, use the gripper snap tool to connect one socket and one wired prong ring to a conductive fabric piece about 1" (2.5cm) in from the edge. Repeat with the other conductive fabric piece. Leave the wires to hang loose **(C)**.

4. Hand-sew the conductive fabric pieces to the sponge or foam, one to the top and one to the bottom, with the wires aligned on top of each other **(D)**.

5. Refer to the project's instructions for soldering the switch's wires.

DONUT SWITCH

Like the Pincushion Switch, the Donut Switch is made from a sponge or piece of foam, but instead of needles, it's triggered by a squeeze. The Donut Switch has a hole in it, so when pressed it pushes the two conductive pieces together to make a connection.

[MATERIALS & TOOLS]

Sponge or foam (type and size is indicated in the project's materials list)

Conductive fabric (size indicated in the projects material list)

Electrical wire

Gripper snaps, 2 sockets size 16 or 19

2 prong rings

Solder

All-purpose thread in any color

Core tools (page 106)

....

1. Cut two pieces of conductive fabric and the foam/sponge into the shape indicated by the project's instructions. Cut a hole in the middle of the foam/sponge with an X-Acto knife, leaving a 1" (2.5cm) perimeter if you're using a pottery sponge and a 2" (5cm) perimeter if you're using foam **(E)**.

2. Cut two 7" (18cm) lengths of wire and strip both ends. Then, follow the instructions on page 111 for soldering one wire to each gripper snap prong ring.

3. Next, use the gripper snap tool to connect one socket and one wired prong ring to a conductive fabric piece about 1" (2.5cm) in from the edge. Repeat with the other conductive piece. Leave the wires to hang loose **(F)**.

4. Hand-sew the conductive fabric pieces to the sponge or foam, one to the top and one to the bottom, with the wires aligned on top of one another **(G)**.

5. Refer to your project's instructions for soldering the wires of the switch.

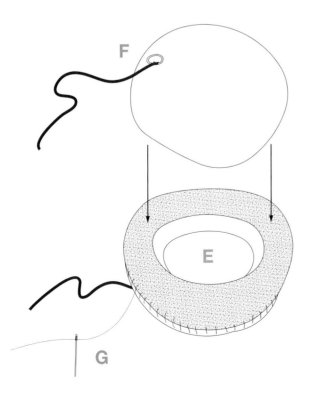

LED BEAD

LED Beads are like tiny lighted sequins you can sew directly onto any creation with conductive thread. You can make them in two different ways: using a surface mount (SMD) LED or a 3mm round LED. If you love working with small things and are familiar with jewelry making, go ahead with the SMD LED Bead; if not, try the round LED Bead.

SMD LED version

These are made from surface mount LEDs soldered to a couple of silver beads. Since they are teeny tiny, get your hands steady and ready for some delicate handiwork.

[MATERIALS & TOOLS]

Surface mount LED (page 103)

2 silver beads—real silver, not just silver-colored

Conductive thread (length indicated in the project's materials list or instructions)

Jewelry wire or fine-tipped tweezers

3-volt coin battery (page 102)

Core tools (page 106)

....

1. On a nonconductive and safe surface, flip your LED to expose the metal contacts on the back side. Apply just a dab of solder to each metal contact. Make sure your soldering iron tip is very clean or it won't stick.

2. Solder one silver bead lengthwise to each LED contact (A) using one of the following two methods:

✳ **TIP:** In order for the bead to stick to the metal surface you must have a clean soldering iron tip. If it is not clean and the bead keeps sticking to the tip instead of the contact, you may have to replace the tip.

using tweezers   Hold a bead next to a metal contact with tweezers. Use a soldering iron to reheat the solder that is already on the contact and carefully apply the bead to the contact. Make sure you solder the bead, not the tweezers (B)! Repeat with the other contact.

✳ **TIP:** The tweezers may become hot due to the soldering iron. You can protect your hands by wrapping the handle in electrical tape or duct tape.

using jewelry wire or thread   String a silver bead with jewelry wire. Hold both ends of the wire in one hand and the soldering iron in the other. Place the bead next to a metal contact. Use a soldering iron to reheat the solder that is already on the contact and carefully apply the bead to the contact (C). Repeat with the other contact.

3. Wait for each bead to cool down then check. If it is loose, remove it and redo step 2.

4. Put your newly made LED Bead onto a 3-volt coin battery as illustrated (D). If it lights up, the contact touching the [–] side of the battery is also the [–] side of your LED Bead. Mark it with a black permanent marker. If it doesn't light up, flip the LED Bead and it should work now; mark the [–] side.

Round LED version

The round LED Bead is larger than the SMD version, but it's easier to make and requires no soldering at all.

[MATERIALS & TOOLS]

3mm LED in color of your choosing (page 103)

....

1. Mark the outside edge of the LED dome with a black permanent marker to indicate the [–] side.

2. Using your jewelry pliers, twist the [+] and [–] legs of the LED into a spiral as illustrated (E). You are done!

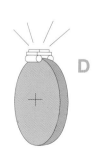

B

A

C

D

E

VIBRATING MOTOR SET

The motion and sensation created by a vibrating motor can add fun and surprise to your switch craft. To add vibrations to a project, you'll need a motor, a battery, and a place to house them. One of the easiest and cheapest ways to get these is to harness parts from a used electric toothbrush and a used lip balm.

[MATERIALS & TOOLS]

Oral-B Pulsar electric toothbrush (you may recycle a used one)

Two 3" (7.5cm) lengths of electrical wire, one red and one black

Plastic lip balm tube, such as a container of ChapStick

AAA battery holder (page 102)

AAA battery (this can be found inside the toothbrush)

Rubber band

Core tools (page 106)

. . . .

1. Inspect your new or used Oral-B Pulsar to find the seam on the handle; it's located where the top and bottom pieces of the toothbrush join. Using two pairs of pliers—one holding the top piece, the other the bottom—firmly twist open the toothbrush counterclockwise. Discard the bottom piece.

2. You should see the tail end of a AAA battery and a metal brace protruding from the toothbrush opening. Hold your toothbrush in one hand, and simultaneously grip the battery and the brace using pliers in the other hand. Carefully but firmly, pull the battery and the brace out of the toothbrush and discard the toothbrush.

3. What you have is a plastic molding with a motor on one end and a metal brace holding a battery on the other. Remove the battery and clip away the battery brace using a wire cutter or a pair of strong scissors (A).

⚠️ **CAUTION:** Beware of the sharp metal edge caused by cutting. Don't hurt yourself!

4. In the middle of the plastic molding is a lever, which was the switch of the toothbrush. Gently remove it to reveal a metal plate underneath (B). If there is some grease on the plate, clean it up with a Q-tip or cloth.

5. Cut and strip two 3" (7.5cm) long wires, preferably one in red and one in black. Look closely at the molding and you will notice two metal plates on opposite sides of the motor, each soldered to a wire from the motor. Solder your red wire onto the metal plate connected to the red motor wire—this is the **[+]** wire. Solder the other wire to the opposite metal plate—this is your **[–]** wire. To prevent vibrations from loosening the soldered wires, apply hot glue liberally to secure both solder joints.

6. Remove and set aside the cap of your lip balm. With a pair of pliers, pull out the bottom rotary dial from the lip balm. This should cause any unused portion of your lip balm stick, along with its base, to fall out. If it doesn't fall out, shake it out, and clean out the container. Throw away the bottom dial.

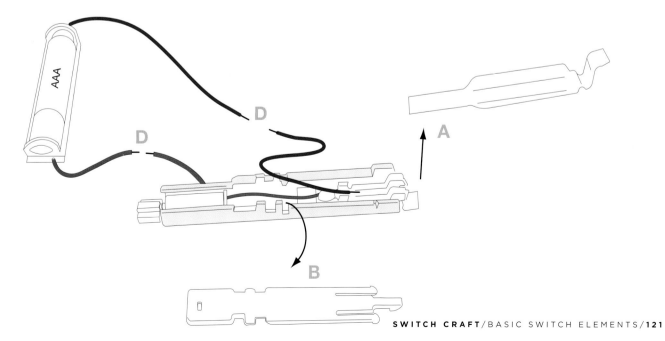

7. Insert the motor molding piece into the lip balm tube with the motor facing toward the top and the wires sticking out of the bottom hole. Adjust the position of the molding piece to keep the motor off center (the more off-center the motor, the more intense the vibrations) but not so much that the eccentric weight on top of the motor would hit the tube or the cap when rotating. The motor head must be allowed to spin freely to work properly (C). Once you find a good spot, apply hot glue liberally to secure the motor casing to the tube. Be mindful not to put glue on the motor or anywhere that may block the rotation of the motor weight.

8. Solder your [–] wire from the newly made motor tube to the black wire from the AAA battery holder (D on previous page). Test the motor by placing a battery in the holder and then temporarily touching the tips of the two exposed red [+]

wires together. If it doesn't vibrate, check your battery and all soldering joints.

9. Once the motor is working properly, insulate the solder joints using electrical tape or hot glue. Put the cap back on and hot glue the bottom hole of the motor tube closed for soundproofing. Use a rubber band to tie together the battery holder and the motor tube (E).

10. Refer to your project instructions for the type of switch to use and how to wire it from this point on.

✳ **TIP:** Visit the book's companion website, www.iheartswitch.com/switchcraft, for step-by-step photos of the toothbrush motor instructions.

CALL INDICATOR SET

The call indicator set lights up whenever you have an incoming call. It works by detecting the radio signal from your phone's antenna, and lets you know there is a call with a flash of light.

[MATERIALS & TOOLS]

Three flashing cell phone charms (see below)
Jeweler's/watchmaker's mini flathead
  screwdriver
Four 2″ (5cm) lengths of electrical wire: one red,
  one black, two blue
Core tools (page 106)

FLASHING CELL-PHONE CHARM

You probably have seen it before: The mobile phone strap starts flashing sparkly lights whenever there is an incoming call. Now you can incorporate it into your own designs. Pick yours up from a local or online store selling cell-phone accessories. Please note that certain phone models may not be able to trigger the flashing. What's more, the chance of getting a non-working charm can be high because these are cheaply made. Always try before you buy.

1. Use your screwdriver to pry open the back of the plastic charm casing and take out the circuit. It should look like a tiny circular sandwich, with a circuit board on top, batteries in the middle, and a metal plate on the bottom. The circuit board and the metal plate are connected by two metal braces.

2. Remove the batteries (A). Pay attention to what side of the battery is touching the bottom metal plate: If the [−] side of your battery is touching the metal plate, continue to step 3. If yours is the opposite ([+] side touching the bottom piece), the [+] and [−] indicated in the following steps and illustrations are reversed.

3. Snip off one metal brace completely. Cut the other brace in the middle (B). Carefully bend the metal piece that is still left on the circuit side out flat with needle-nose pliers. This is your [−] connection (C). Now flip the charm over. You should see a metal wire or metallic coating on the bottom of the circuit board (where the battery was touching). This is your [+] connection.

4. Repeat the above steps with the other two charms.

5. With their [+] sides facing upward, position these three charms in an arrangement that fits inside the designated area of your project.

6. Cut and strip one 2″ (5cm) red wire, one 2″ (5cm) black wire, and two other colored wires (we used blue) long enough to go between the charms. Following the illustration closely, create a serial chain of charms by soldering your wires to the charms as shown (D).

7. You are done. The two unused ends of the red and black wires are the [+] and [−] connections of your newly made Call Indicator Set.

PATTERNS, SCHEMATICS, AND TEMPLATES

Each pattern includes a magnification percentage, and, for additional help, many contain an arrow that should be 2″ (5cm) long when the pattern is magnified to the correct size. Since the patterns for Cushion Brite (page 132) and Galaxy Carrier 802.11 (page 133) are made of simple shapes, the measurements are included on the schematics so that you can draft your own pattern using a ruler. The following patterns will need to be photocopied and enlarged to the appropriate size before you pin them to your fabric. In small quantities, for personal use, you are free to make photocopies from this book.

ANTENNA BAG PATTERN

Photocopy at 400% magnification

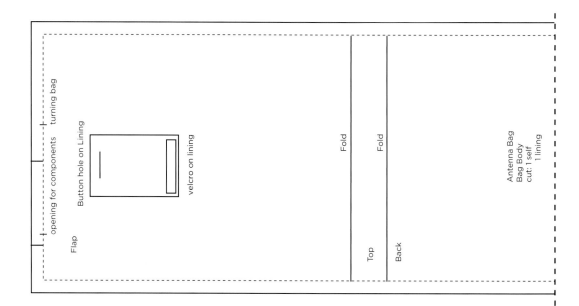

PATTERN LEGEND

⊗ Snaps

○ Magnets

⬦ Alignment in middle of fabric

▼ ◆ Alignment/Matching to fabric edges

△ Notching

- - - - - Seamline

───── Cutting or Clipping Line

───── Fold lines

············ Placement of non-fabric objects

───── Placement of fabric objects

◄────► Corner placement and alignment

∘───∘ Darts

◄────► Grainline

▨ Cutouts

⋈⋈⋈⋈ Zipper

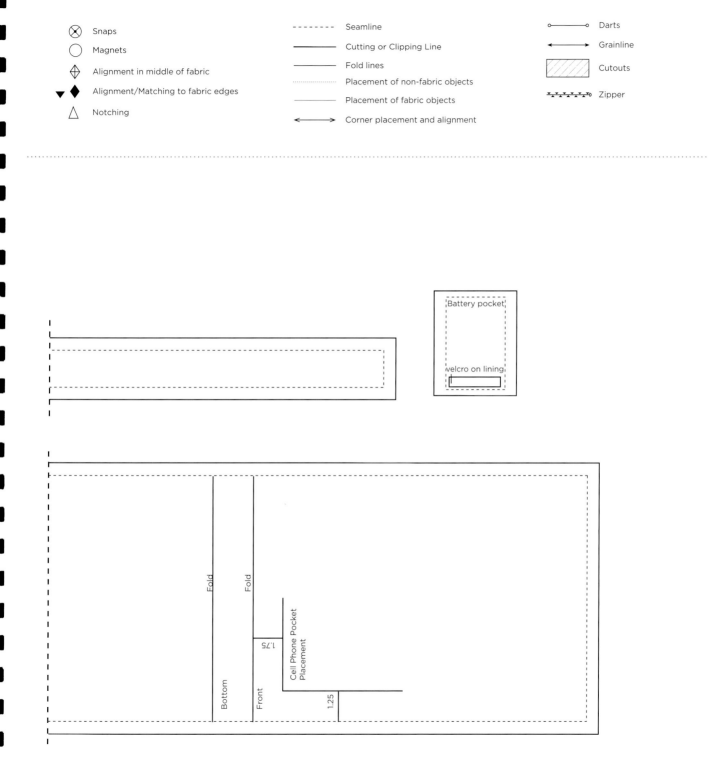

Battery pocket

velcro on lining

Fold

Fold

Bottom

Front

Cell Phone Pocket Placement

1.75

1.25

URBAN BLASTER PATTERN
Photocopy at 285% magnification

URBAN BLASTER BUCKET

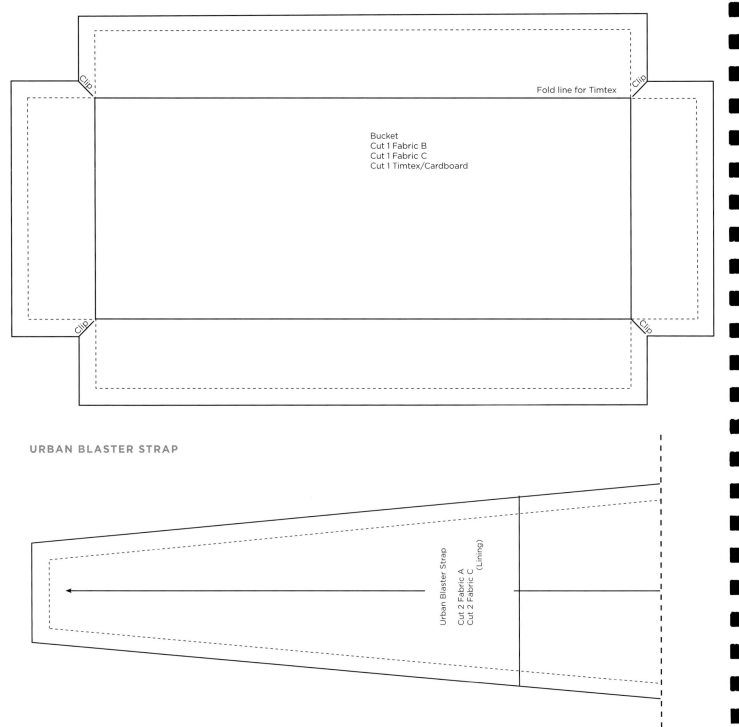

Fold line for Timtex

Clip

Clip

Clip

Clip

Bucket
Cut 1 Fabric B
Cut 1 Fabric C
Cut 1 Timtex/Cardboard

URBAN BLASTER STRAP

Urban Blaster Strap

Cut 2 Fabric A
Cut 2 Fabric C (Lining)

URBAN BLASTER FRONT POCKET

Photocopy at 285% magnification

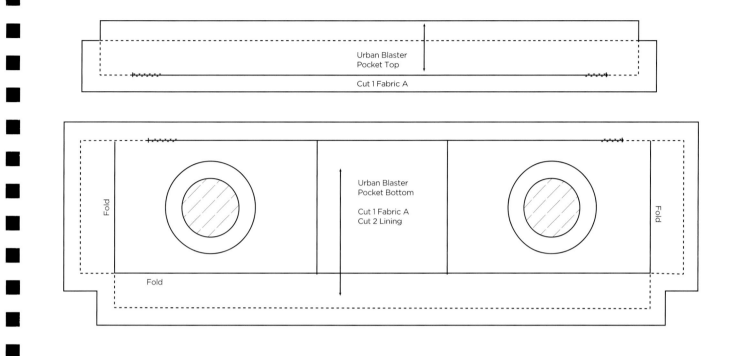

Urban Blaster
Pocket Top

Cut 1 Fabric A

Fold

Urban Blaster
Pocket Bottom

Cut 1 Fabric A
Cut 2 Lining

Fold

Fold

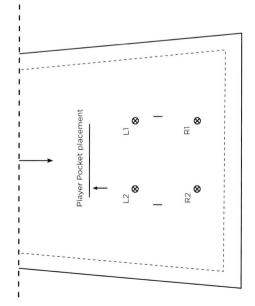

Player Pocket placement

L1   R1

L2   R2

URBAN BLASTER DIVIDER

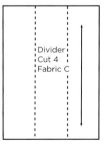

Divider
Cut 4
Fabric C

URBAN BLASTER BODY

Photocopy at 285% magnification

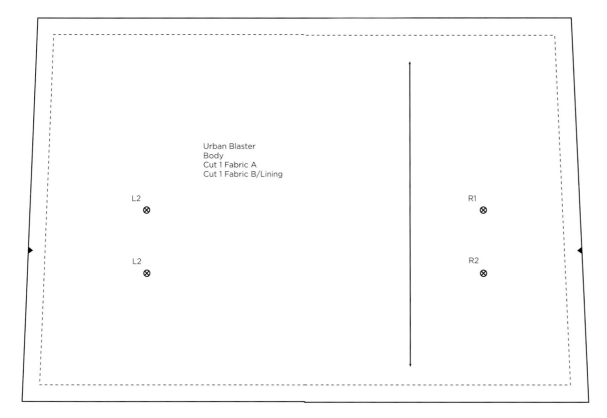

Urban Blaster
Body
Cut 1 Fabric A
Cut 1 Fabric B/Lining

L2

L2

R1

R2

FIREFLY BRACELET

Photocopy at 200% magnification

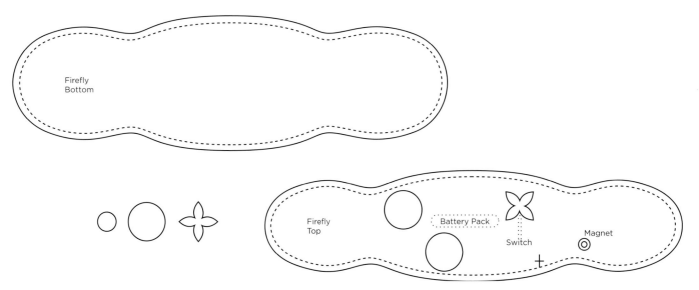

Firefly
Bottom

Firefly
Top

Battery Pack

Switch

Magnet

CATCH ME IF YOU CAN PATTERN

Photocopy at 150% magnification

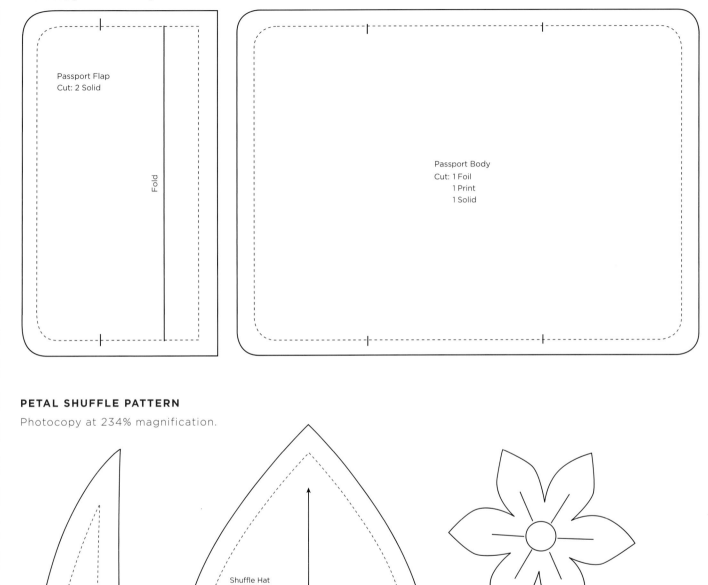

Passport Flap
Cut: 2 Solid

Fold

Passport Body
Cut: 1 Foil
1 Print
1 Solid

PETAL SHUFFLE PATTERN

Photocopy at 234% magnification.

Shuffle Hat
Brim
Cut: 2 Fabric
Cut: 1 Timtex

Shuffle Hat
Panel
Cut: 4 Fabric
Cut: 4 Lining

Pocket Placement

Shuffle Hat
Pocket
Cut: 1 Fabric

iHOODIE PATTERN

Photocopy at 350% magnification

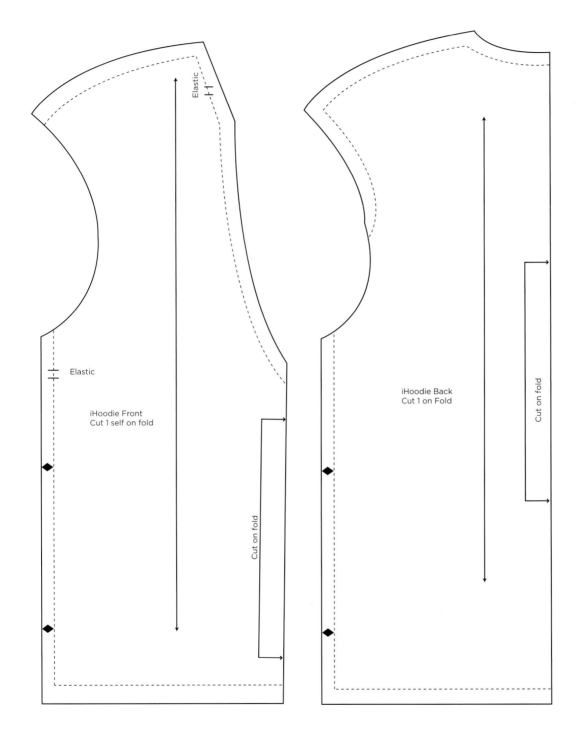

Elastic

Elastic

iHoodie Front
Cut 1 self on fold

Cut on fold

iHoodie Back
Cut 1 on Fold

Cut on fold

iHOODIE PATTERN

Photocopy at 350% magnification

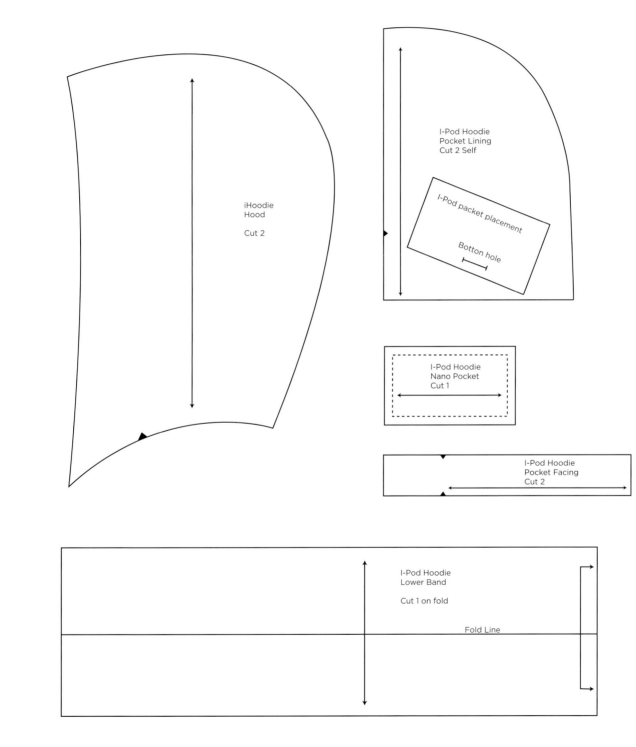

iHoodie
Hood

Cut 2

I-Pod Hoodie
Pocket Lining
Cut 2 Self

I-Pod packet placement

Botton hole

I-Pod Hoodie
Nano Pocket
Cut 1

I-Pod Hoodie
Pocket Facing
Cut 2

I-Pod Hoodie
Lower Band

Cut 1 on fold

Fold Line

CUSHION BRITE SCHEMATIC

Below are the measurements to create the pattern for Cushion Brite. The measurements include the ½″ (13mm) seam allowance.

To draw the 17″ (43cm) circle, tie a piece of string to a pin, make a knot with a loop 8½″ (21.5cm) from the pin, and stick the pin into the center of the circle. Then insert the tip of a pencil into the loop, and, keeping the thread taut, move it around the pin in a circle.

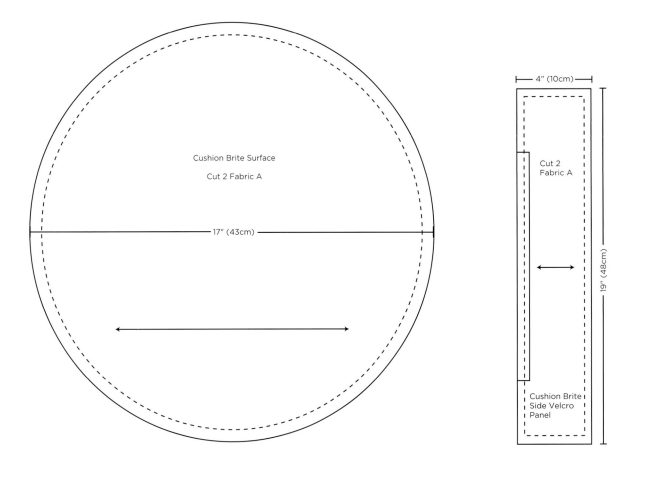

Cushion Brite Surface
Cut 2 Fabric A

17″ (43cm)

4″ (10cm)

Cut 2
Fabric A

19″ (48cm)

Cushion Brite
Side Velcro
Panel

34³/₈″ (87.31cm)

Cushion Brite
Side Panel

Cut 1 Fabric A

4″ (10cm)

GALAXY CARRIER 802.11 SCHEMATIC

Below are the measurements to create the pattern to fit a 1" x 14" x 9 ½" (2.5cm x 35.5cm x 24.4cm) laptop. The measurements include the ½" (13mm) seam allowance. Change the height and width according to the size of your computer.

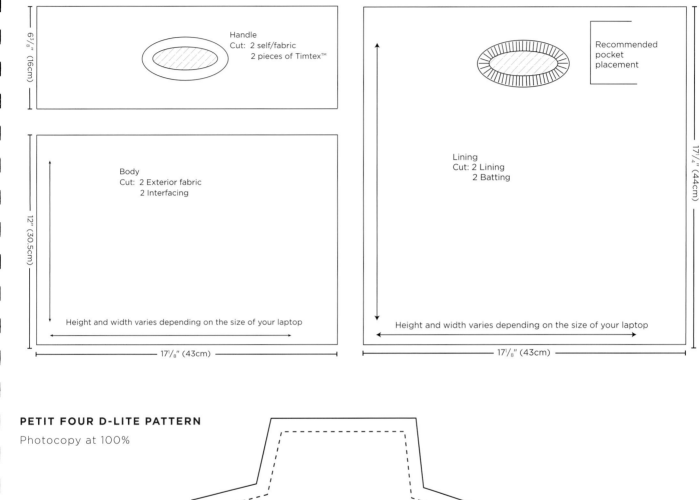

6³/₈" (16cm)

Handle
Cut: 2 self/fabric
2 pieces of Timtex™

12" (30.5cm)

Body
Cut: 2 Exterior fabric
2 Interfacing

Height and width varies depending on the size of your laptop

17¹/₈" (43cm)

Recommended pocket placement

17¹/₄" (44cm)

Lining
Cut: 2 Lining
2 Batting

Height and width varies depending on the size of your laptop

17¹/₈" (43cm)

PETIT FOUR D-LITE PATTERN

Photocopy at 100%

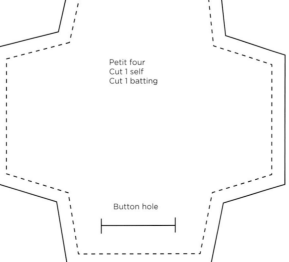

Petit four
Cut 1 self
Cut 1 batting

Button hole

PILLOW TALK PATTERN

Photocopy at 400% magnification

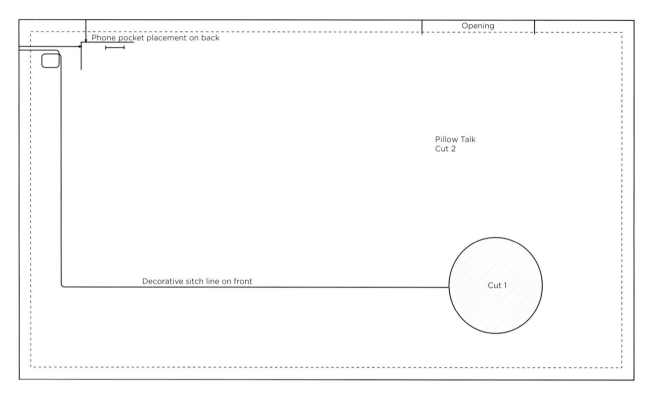

Opening

Phone pocket placement on back

Pillow Talk
Cut 2

Cut 1

Decorative sitch line on front

MII DOLL PATTERN

Photocopy at 385% magnification

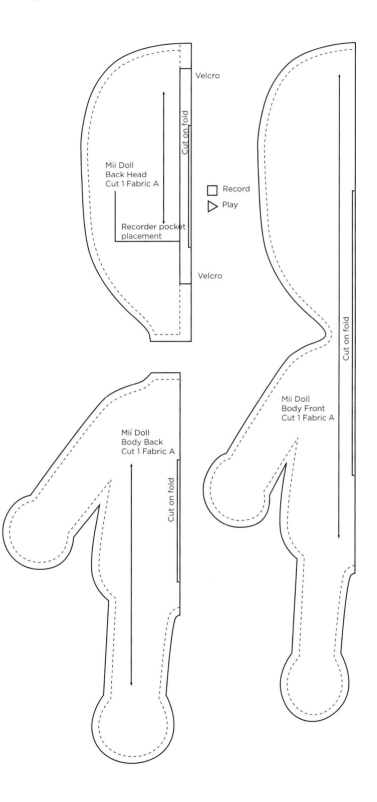

Velcro

Cut on fold

Mii Doll
Back Head
Cut 1 Fabric A

Record

Play

Recorder pocket
placement

Velcro

Cut on fold

Mii Doll
Body Front
Cut 1 Fabric A

Mií Doll
Body Back
Cut 1 Fabric A

Cut on fold

GADGET GLOVES PATTERN

Photocopy at 200% magnification

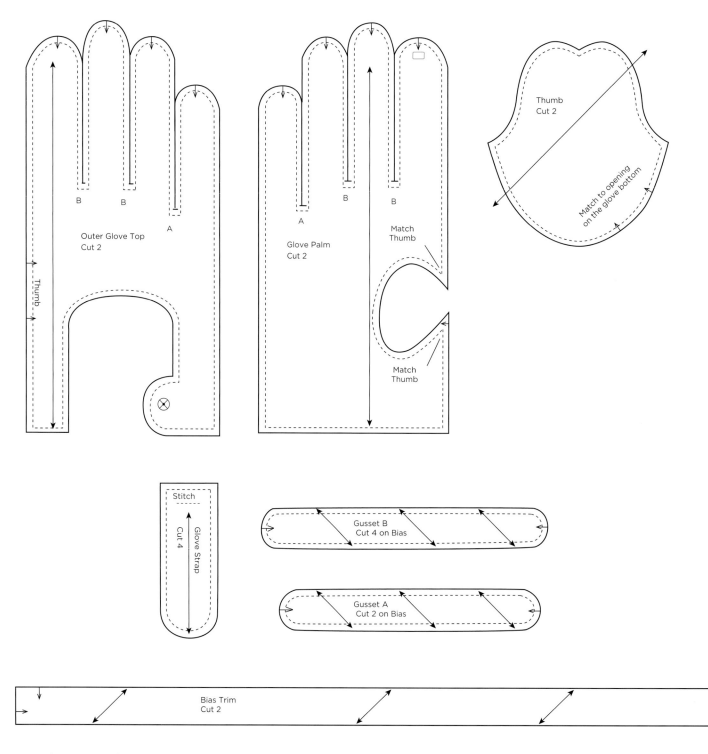

Outer Glove Top
Cut 2

Thumb

B   B   A

Glove Palm
Cut 2

B   B   A

Match
Thumb

Match
Thumb

Thumb
Cut 2

Match to opening
on the glove bottom

Stitch

Glove Strap
Cut 4

Gusset B
Cut 4 on Bias

Gusset A
Cut 2 on Bias

Bias Trim
Cut 2

AROMATHERAPY SACHET PATTERN

Photocopy at 200%

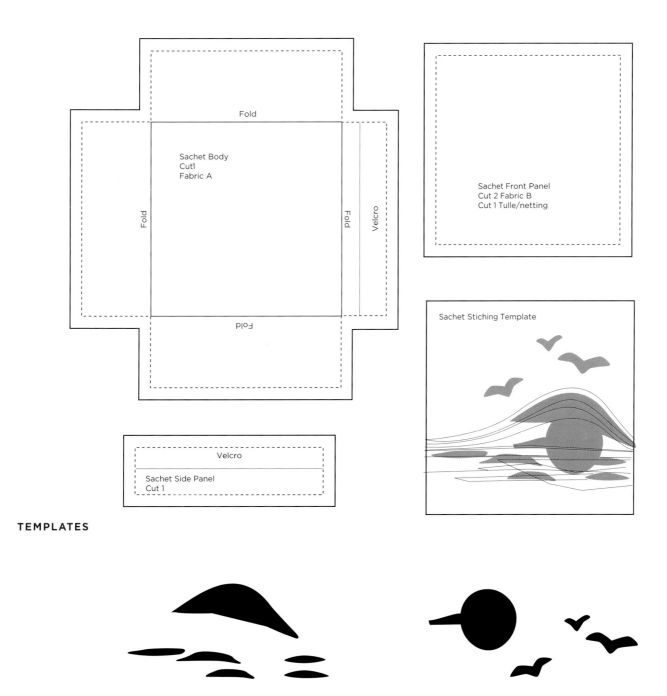

Fold

Sachet Body
Cut1
Fabric A

Fold

Fold

Velcro

Fold

Sachet Front Panel
Cut 2 Fabric B
Cut 1 Tulle/netting

Sachet Stiching Template

Velcro

Sachet Side Panel
Cut 1

TEMPLATES

VOODOODOLL PATTERN
Photocopy at 175% magnification

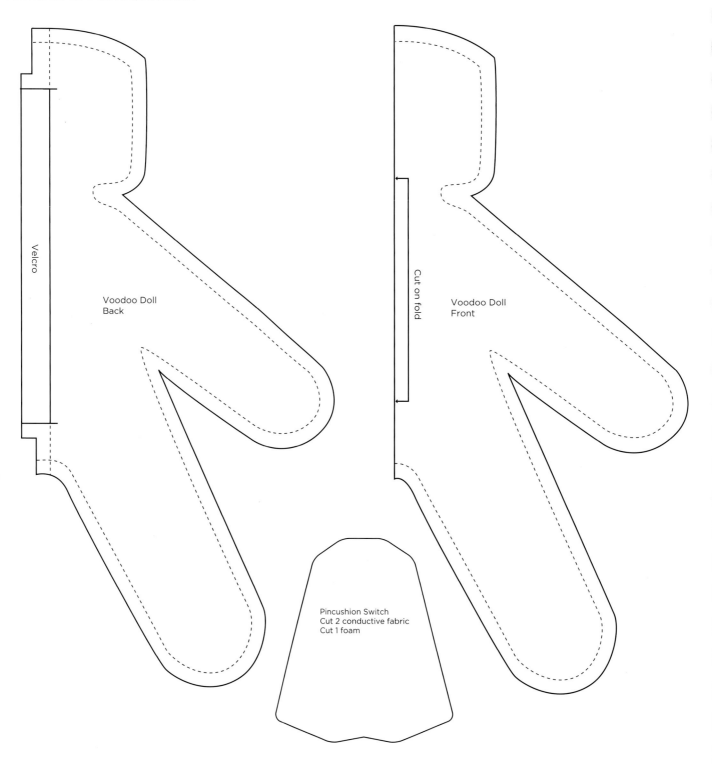

Velcro

Voodoo Doll
Back

Cut on fold

Voodoo Doll
Front

Pincushion Switch
Cut 2 conductive fabric
Cut 1 foam

SEAFOOD CAT TOY PATTERN
Photocopy at 200% magnification

Squid Tentacles

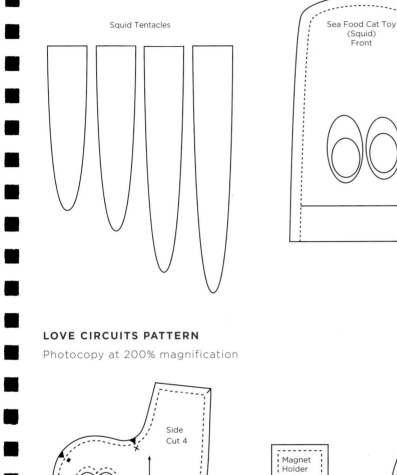

Sea Food Cat Toy
(Squid)
Front

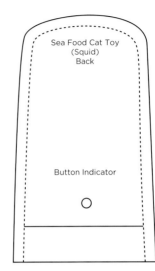

Sea Food Cat Toy
(Squid)
Back

Button Indicator

LOVE CIRCUITS PATTERN
Photocopy at 200% magnification

Side
Cut 4

Magnet
Holder
Cut 2

Battery Pocket
Cut 2

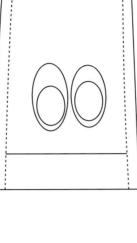

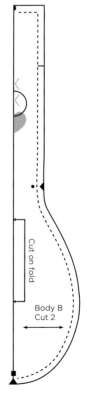

Cut on fold

Body B
Cut 2

Body A
Cut 2

Cut on fold

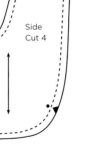

Embroidery on the front
of the Lovies should look
like the designs to the
left. The hearts and x's
should be opposite one
another

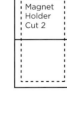

Heart
Cut 2

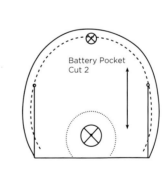

SHINY CLUTCH PATTERN

Photocopy at 300% magnification

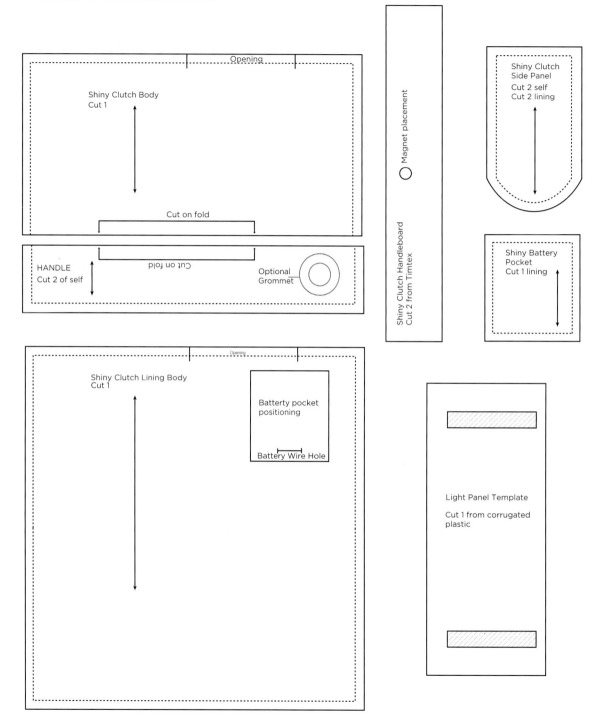

GLOSSARY

Alternating Current (AC): Electrical current that shifts or reverses directions at regular intervals. You'll find this type of electrical current in your home.

Backstitch: To go back over a set of stitches that were just created. It is usually a setting on your sewing machine for stitching in reverse and is used for reinforcing the seam.

Conductivity: The degree to which a material conducts electricity.

Direct Current (DC): Electrical current that flows in one direction only. You'll find this type of electrical current in batteries.

Hand-stitch: Sewing by hand using a needle and thread. This can be done in any stitch type.

Inverter: An inverter changes, or "inverts," a digital number from one to the other. In the case of *Switch Craft*, inverters are electronic units that convert DC power to AC power.

Normally-closed (NC): A circuit that is "connected" or "closed" when in its static state. When it is opened the connection is broken. It's like a front door, which is usually closed when at rest.

Normally-open: A circuit that is not connected and stays open when in its static state. When it is closed the circuit is connected. This is like a necklace: When it lays on the table it is unclasped, but it works (can be worn) when it is clasped together.

Parallel: Circuits that are in parallel share a common point at each end, like people holding hands that stand across from one another. These are not in a series and the current passes through components equally and at the same time.

Polarity: Polarity is the electricity that runs through a component in one direction, usually from **[+]** to **[−]** Components that have polarity include LEDs and batteries.

Running stitch: A series of stitches that run in a row through the fabric without touching.

Series: A line of components, usually batteries or LEDs, which are lined up in a row like a line of people holding hands. The current from the power passes through each component successively.

Slip stitch: A loose stitch joining multiple layers of fabrics together with an invisible edge.

Whipstitch: A stitch joining multiple layers of fabrics together that is visible on the edge. The stitch runs through the top fabric, then runs to the outside of the secondary fabric on the outside edge.

RESOURCES

This list is included for your convenience and certainly is not exhaustive or exclusive. To make this book more universal, only stores that have an online presence or national chains are mentioned. However, we do support local businesses and welcome you to share with other readers where to find things in your neighborhood by leaving messages on the book's companion site. There you may also find part numbers or further information for specific products and electronic components.

GENERAL ARTS & CRAFTS SUPPLIES

Michaels
www.michaels.com

Jo-Ann Fabric and Craft Stores
www.joann.com

Pearl Paint
www.pearlpaint.com

Mood Fabric
www.moodfabric.com

NY Elegant Fabrics
www.nyelegantfabrics.com

Marimekko
www.marimekko.com/eng

Alexander Henry Fabrics
www.ahfabrics.com

Paron Fabrics
www.paronfabrics.com

IKEA
www.ikea.com

B&J Fabrics
www.bandjfabrics.com

Purl Soho
www.purlsoho.com

The City Quilter
www.cityquilter.com

J&O Fabrics
www.jandofabrics.com/fabric-store.asp

Discount Fabric
www.discountfabric.com

Repro Depot
www.reprodepot.com

TRIMMINGS & NOTIONS

M&J Trimmings
www.mjtrim.com

Botani Trimmings
www.botaniusa.com

Trim Fabric
www.trimfabric.com

JEWELRY MAKING AND BEADING SUPPLIES

Toho Shoji
www.tohoshoji-ny.com

Fire Mountain Gems and Beads
www.firemountaingems.com

Jewelry Supply Inc.
www.jewelrysupply.com

CONDUCTIVE THREADS AND FABRICS

Lamésaver
members.shaw.ca/ubik/thread/order.html

LessEMF
www.lessemf.com/fabric.html

BlockEMF
www.blockemf.com

Spark Fun Electronics
www.sparkfun.com

GENERAL ELECTRONIC SUPPLIES
For tools, wires, switches, LEDs, etc.

Radio Shack
www.radioshack.com

Jameco
www.jameco.com

All Electronics
www.allelectronics.com

Digi-Key
www.digikey.com

Minute Man Electronics
www.minute-man.com

Electronic Goldmine
www.goldmine-elec.com

SparkFun
www.sparkfun.com

Action Electronics
www.action-electronics.com

ELECTRONIC PRODUCTS
For low-priced headsets, speakers, keychain recorders, cell phone charms, etc.

ebay
www.ebay.com

Amazon
www.amazon.com

Google Product Search
www.google.com/products

HARDWARE

The Home Depot
www.homedepot.com

Lowe's
www.lowes.com

LEDS

Super Bright LEDs
www.superbrightleds.com
See also General Electronic Supplies

BATTERIES

Microbattery.com
www.microbattery.com

CheapBatteries.com
www.cheapbatteries.com

EL WIRES & DRIVERS

Cool Neon
www.coolneon.com

Live Wire
www.elbestbuy.com

VibeLights
www.vibelights.com

WorldAglow
www.coollightwest.com

PUSH-ACTIVATED SOUND KITS

Build-A-Bear Workshop
www.buildabear.com/shop

The Bear Mill
www.thebearmillinc.com/retailstore

Made with Kisses and Hugs
stores.madewithkissesandhugs.net

REFERENCES

We were inspired by a number of people and projects for *Switch Craft*. Take some time to look, do a web search, and find out about them yourself. If we missed anyone in this list, drop by iheartswitch.com/switchcraft and let us know.

LED Bead
LED Sequins, Leah Buechley

Dancing Queen Skirt
Fire Skirt, Laura Cesari
Enlighted Designs, Janet Hansen

Cushion Brite
LightSleeper, Rachel Wingfield and Mathias Gmachl of Loop.pH

Shiny Clutch
Sun Trap Solar Illuminated Bag, Rosanna Kilfedder

Firefly Bracelet
Wearable Light Cuff, Syuzi Pakhchyan of SparkLab
Starlights, Alice Tseng-Planas

Pillow Talk
whiSpiral, Elena Corchero and Stefan Agamanolis

Lovie Circuts
Hug Jackets, Despina Papadopoulos of 5050ltd

Urban Blaster
Fendi Ghetto Blaster, Francesca Granata

Catch Me If You Can
RFID Pocket Replacement, Mikey Sklar

Gadget Gloves
iPod Mittins, Leah Culver

Mii Doll
www.miiware.com

VooDooDoll
Voodoodoll, Alice Planas

GENERAL REFERENCES

How Stuff Works
www.howstuffworks.com

Wikipedia
www.wikipedia.com

Battery University
www.batteryuniversity.com

Boom Box Museum
www.pocketcalculatorshow.com/boombox

ASPCA
www.aspca.org

ONLINE INSPIRATION

AEO Lab with Elise Co
www.aeolab.com/

5050 LTD.
www.5050ltd.com

Burda Style
www.burdastyle.com

Coquette
coquette.blogs.com

Craft Technology Group
http://l3d.cs.colorado.edu/~ctg/

Cute Circuit
www.cutecircuit.com

Design Sponge
www.designspongeonline.com

Etsy
www.etsy.com

Fashion Technology Research Consortium
www.fashionabletechnology.org

Geek Sugar
www.geeksugar.com

Instructables
www.instructables.com

Jean-Baptiste Labrune
http://insitu.lri.fr/~labrune/

Leah Buechley
http://www.cs.colorado.edu/~buechley

Pop Gadget
www.popgadget.net

Sew News
www.sewnews.com

Techie Diva
www.techiediva.com

21f Organization
www.twenty1f.com

We Make Money Not Art
www.we-make-money-not-art.com

XS Labs
www.xslabs.net

FURTHER READING
Books

Marvin, Carolyn. *When Old Technologies Were New: Thinking About Electric Communication in the Late Nineteenth Century*. NY: Oxford, 1990.

Quinn, Bradley. *Techno Fashion*. UK: Berg Publishers, 2002.

Reader's Digest editors. *New Complete Guide to Sewing (Reader's Digest)*. NY: Reader's Digest, 2002.

Eng, Diana and Natalie Zee Drieu. *TechStyle: Create Wired Wearables and Geeky Gear*. NJ: Wiley, 2008

Vogue Knitting magazine. *Vogue Sewing: Revised and Updated*. NY: Sixth&Spring Books, 2006.

Magazines

Craft magazine

Make magazine

Readymade magazine

ACKNOWLEDGMENTS

This book would not be possible without the help and support of the following people and organizations.

Thanks first of all to Kate McKean of the Howard Morheim Literary Agency, and the Potter Craft team: Rosy Ngo, Erin Slonaker, Chi Ling Moy, La Tricia Watford, Jen Graham, and all of you at Potter Craft who made this book possible. Also Heather Weston for the photographs, Hiromi Sugie for the technical illustrations, Ashlee Rudert for sewing and making the majority of our patterns, and Lauren Ann Niles for prop styling.

We too would like to thank Parsons The New School for Design's Communication Design & Technology Department, and the Design & Management Department for providing us with talent and support, Phil Torrone of *Make* magazine for sharing space with us, and the people at Etsy Labs.

Christopher Stewart Arnold III, thank you for your endless hours of work to help bring this book to life. Lauren Miller and Christina Schoen, thank you for your help in shaping the book early on. Leah Buechley for your feedback and suggestions. Also thank you Julia Howe and Matthew Mohr for your input and assistance.

CONTRIBUTING DESIGNERS

Agnieszka Gasparska is the founder of New York City design studio Kiss Me I'm Polish. Her clients have included the National Recording Academy, Jazz at Lincoln Center, the Japan Society, Bloomberg, and Fischerspooner. She lives in Brooklyn and, come summertime, can often be spotted in the wee hours of the morning sneaking out of her fourth-floor walk-up with a nine-foot surfboard.

Kim Gilbert loves color and simple composition. She designs her own line of modern earrings (www.kgearthings.com) and is a color designer for a sneaker company. She graduated from the Maryland Institute College of Art and lives in Portland, Oregon, with her genius cat, Alan.

Sylwia Jas has been designing since she was eight years old. After attending fashion school in Poland she started her own company. Wanting more exposure, she moved to Italy for four years and now resides in New York City. Sylwia's enthusiasm for eccentric design is inspired by her many travels around the world.

Jennifer Liang, a native New Yorker, was born and raised in Rego Park, Queens. She attended Boston University, and after receiving her BS in Communications, headed back to NYC where she worked at a digital advertising agency. Ms. Liang likes anything to do with textiles, working with her hands, and collecting vintage clothing and furniture.

Pum Photjananuwat loves arts and crafts, which she got from her mother. Her designs are inspired by nature, the chaos of a big city, and her curiosity of technology. Born and raised in Bangkok, Pum has lived in New York City since 1999, where she works as an architectural lighting designer.

CONSULTING DESIGNERS

Chris Ritchie
Claudia Bernett
Allison Conner
Aya Karpinska
Karen Lee
Jacky Myint
Alice Planas
Gretta Krechmaras
Millie Sensat
Caitlin Lazia
Chia Jung Chang

Ivona Zdravevska
Soyoung Park
Youn Jin Park
Kate Hartman
Becky Herritage
Stephen Pandolfi
Nasiya Reid

SEWING & PATTERNMAKING

Daun Fallon
Lauren Munger
Rika Minhee Yamamoto
Anna Zeman

ASSISTANTS & INTERNS

Joey Sweeny
Shannon O'Neill
Julia Vallera
Jason Hare

MODELS & STYLISTS

Sam Giordano
Julia Joseph
Lauren Munger
Jennifer Liang
Ceaser "licky chops" Lewis (the dog)
Ms. Ferdinand (the cat)

LOCATIONS

David Land and Rumaan Alam's apartment
Vespa store in SoHo, Manhattan
Superfine in DUMBO, Brooklyn

Last but not least, to our families and friends who supported us throughout the making of the book: **Thank you.**